MY
COUNTRY
ROOTS

**THE ULTIMATE
MP3 GUIDE
TO AMERICA'S
ORIGINAL
OUTSIDER
MUSIC**

D1510110

New York Times Best-Selling Author
ALICE RANDALL
WITH CARTER LITTLE & COURTNEY LITTLE

Foreword by **GEORGE JONES**

MP3
HAND
BOOK

**NAKED
INK**

Published by Naked Ink, a Division of The General Trade Book Group of Thomas Nelson Publishers, Inc., P.O. Box 141000, Nashville, Tennessee, 37214.

ISBN-10: 15955558608

ISBN-13: 978-1-59555-860-2

Printed in the United States of America.

06 07 08 09 — 9 8 7 6 5 4 3 2 1

A Word Of Caution:

Downloading or transferring music without proper permission or payment is illegal and punishable by law. The authors of *My Country Roots* believe you should "pay to play," whether it's a song or an album, and they intend for this book to be used solely in conjunction with the practice of legal downloading. There are very few songs that may not be available for digital download online at this time. So, if you want to add Garth Brooks to a list, or someone else you may not be able to find, you must purchase their albums through the appropriate online or local retailers and then transfer those recordings to your computer. Show your support of the hard-working songwriters and musicians who make this music possible. Pay to play. Thank you.

Acknowledgements

The authors would like to thank those people who have kindly contributed their talent and time towards the successful completion of this book, with particular humble thanks to the following: Rebekah J. Whitlock, Bo Spessard, Susan Nadler, John Huie, Rodd Essig, Evelyn Schriver, Austin Gray, Lindsey Jamieson, Caroline Randall Williams, Ralph Murphy, D.K. Barton, Vivian Williams, Mimi Oka, David Ewing, Amanda Little, and Sophie Simmons.

Dedication

"It's been rough and rocky traveling but I'm finally standing upright on the ground."
—Willie Nelson, "Me and Paul"

To Frank Little, who was lovingly raised on this music and departed us wishing for this book.

And to the songwriters we have known and loved: Steve Earle and Allison Moorer; Bob McDill and Bobby Braddock; Mark Sanders and Marshall Chapman; Ray Kennedy and Robert Jetton; Don Shlitz and Matraca Berg and Harry Stinson; Guy Clark and David Olney; Kevin Welch and Willis Alan Ramsey and J.C. Crowley; Bob Doyle and Garth Brooks and Pat Alger; Marcus Hummon and Jeff Hanna and Bruce Bouton; Tia Sillers and Radney Foster; John Hartford and Anders Osborne; Jonathan Long and Rowland Stebbins; Shannon Lawson and Dave Coleman; Michael Merenda and Richard Upchurch; Colin Linden and Carter Wood; Harlan Howard and Mickey Newberry; Amy Grant; Rodney Crowell; Don Schlitz; and Bob Delevante, who took our photograph.

Table of Contents

CONTENTS

Introduction

Country music. Is it . . .

A hard music for a hard people, or cliché music for a sentimental people? Do all country songs sound alike, or is country music as diverse as the nation that birthed it? Three chords and the truth, or reverb, synthesizers, and platitudes? Intricate psychological, social, and political observations, or rants about Mama, Prison, and Work? Racist, or class-conscious, or both? A genre heavily influenced by European music, or a genre heavily influenced by African-American instruments, blues progressions, and jazz solos? Warmed over rock 'n' roll, or birthed from the cradle of Elvis, Jerry Lee Lewis, and Chuck Berry?

Country music is all of the above. Love it or hate it, there's more to this genre than most people recognize. No genre of music deals with a more diverse body of subject matter, provides a more mature perspective, or draws from a wider range of conflicting impulses than Country.

Foreword

This is a kind of last will and testament, except you don't have to wait for me to die to get what's coming to you. I want you to have a big time while I can enjoy knowing you're having a big time.

There are some things you need to remember and some things you need to forget. You learn that in seventy-five years on this earth and fifty-two years in the music business.

Forget they called me No Show Jones. Forget Ralph Emery and T. Tommy Cutrer tagged me "The Possum" after I looked real bad on the *White Lightning* album cover. Forget the drugs and the alcohol and that old story nobody ever got right about me riding to town on a lawn mower to get a drink.

You can even forget that I charted 166 singles. The ladies at Bandit Records, Susan Nadler and Evelyn Shriver, tell me that's more than any artist in any format of music. Forget that, too.

Remember this. Out of those 166 songs, "He Stopped Loving Her Today" is a favorite song of mine. When we first cut it, I thought it was too sad. Fans proved me wrong. "She Thinks I Still Care" and "Walk Through This World With Me" are also favorite songs of mine. When I pass away, let those three recordings be what remains of me on this earth.

But that's not all I leave behind. I got more from seventy-five trips around the sun than the songs I sang. I got the songs I heard and loved.

It started for me when I was seven years old, in the part of east Texas they call the Big Thicket. My daddy got our family a radio, and that's when I first heard "Wabash Cannon Ball" and "The Great Speckle Bird."

I leave you my respect for Roy Acuff. I leave you the thrill it was for me to come to Nashville and work with him, laugh with him, and be sad with him. I leave you the thrill it always was for me to step on the Opry stage with Bill Monroe. Acuff and Monroe—that's the first piece of your inheritance.

The second piece is Hank Williams, Senior. It was back in 1947 or 1948 when I first heard Hank Williams. I flipped over his voice. I still do. My favorite Hank Williams song is "You Win, Again." Use *My Country Roots* to find your way to some Hank Williams you haven't heard in a long time, or to some Hank Williams you have never heard before. Hank Williams's voice is just simply the best.

The last thing I'm leaving you is my respect for Merle Haggard. Merle Haggard is one of the best songwriters who ever lived. Nobody who's ever come after is any better than he is.

I first met Merle Haggard in Bakersfield, California in 1962. We were at the same radio station to promote our records. I was there with "She Thinks I Still Care" and he was there with "Sing Me a Sad Song."

Forty some years later, we're doing a new record this year. He's recording five of my songs and I'm recording five of his. It's going to be a big time. When you download those cuts, you can join the party.

The book you're holding in your hands now, *My Country Roots*, is going to take some of my old friends who died in the twentieth century into the twenty-first. And it's going to take a look at a whole lot of new Country singers and a few living legends. That's why I'm here to tell you about it. This book gives you a new way to find the great pickers, the great singers, and the great songwriters who are my country roots.

I'm a traditionalist. I love the old music. I love the ways we used to record—but legal music downloading is also one of the great things about modern technology.

Fishing in the middle of a lake, a hundred miles from electricity, with a little machine in your hands, you can have a hundred of Acuff's songs, a hundred of Bill Monroe's, a hundred of Hank Williams's, a hundred of Merle Haggard's, a hundred of mine, and whatever else you want to listen to, tucked in your pocket on a mp3 player. But you got to know where to go to find what you like. This book will help with that.

There is nothing in the world like country music. A great country song will tear your heart out. Country songs go with you to work, sit with you when you're crying, slide in the room when you're loving, and hang around in your heart when the loving leaves. A great country record can help turn a body on and will help hold a life together when everything falls apart.

Last September I released a CD called *Hits I Missed and One I Didn't*.... Really and truly that thing started off as something called *Songs I Wished I Had Recorded*. The main thing about that album (I try to say CD, and this is a forward to a book about downloads, but they're all still albums to me), is I wanted to pay my respect to some songs I didn't record: "Funny How Time Slips Away," "Detroit City," "The Blues Man," "Here in the Real World," "If You Gonna Do Me Wrong," "Today I Started

Loving You Again," "On the Other Hand," "Pass Me By," "Skip a Rope," "Too Cold At Home," and "Busted."

Some of these originals, like some of my early hits, started off on vinyl, moved onto eight tracks, then onto cassettes before jumping onto CDs. And now they're somewhere out there waiting to be downloaded. You could have a good time thinking how good it would be to hear my versions alongside the originals.

Used to be only the singer and the band had a playlist and you had to listen to songs in the order they were put on the album. Things change. Sometimes that's a good thing.

I still headline about a hundred shows a year. One of the songs I like to sing when I'm out there on the road is "Who's Gonna Fill Their Shoes." Max D. Barnes and Troy Seals got it just about right. The radio has abandoned our legends. They don't understand there won't be no new Roy Acuff or Hank Williams, or Johnny Cash, or Willie Nelson, or Waylon Jennings, any more than there's going to be a new William Shakespeare. Like the song says, "There's nothing better once you've had the best."

As long as babies cry, hearts break, good times shout, and lonely folk hang their heads; as long as being poor hurts, and loving helps—people all over the world will listen to great Country music.

Welcome to Country cyberspace—the place where songs that have stood the test of time meet the songs fighting to make their way.

I don't need no rocking chair—but I got me an iPod. I hope you put a few of my old friends and old favorites on your new playlists. You could start with the song I leave to my wife, Nancy: "I'm a One Woman Man." That's a part of my legacy that was a long time coming. And it's the last thing I'm leaving you with—living proof that legends and legacies change. And that's the biggest time of all.

George Jones
Franklin, Tennessee
2006

A George Jones Playlist:

She Thinks I Still Care . . . . **George Jones**

One of George Jones's favorite George Jones records.

Walk Through This World with Me . . . . . . **George Jones**

Another favorite of George, by George.

Today I Started Loving You Again . . . . . . **Merle Haggard**

One of George's favorite Haggard songs.

Wabash Cannon Ball . . . . **Roy Acuff**

One of the first songs George heard on the radio. Acuff started playing on the Opry about the same time the Jones family got a radio.

The Window Up Above . . . . **George Jones**

This classic, which is one of the greatest, if not the greatest of all, cheating songs, reveals Jones as a master songwriter who didn't need a co-writer to create a song for the ages. Jones wrote sixteen of his first twenty hits.

Why Baby Why . . . . **George Jones**

George's first big (top five) hit. Jones co-wrote this one with Darrell Edwards.

You Win Again . . . . **Hank Williams**

The other of George's favorite Hank songs.

He Stopped Loving Her Today . . . . **George Jones**

George's biggest song ever, and his all time favorite. "Has to be."

Oh Lonesome Me . . . . **Roy Orbison**

Don Gibson, the songwriter, originally pitched this one to George who passed on it. He still regrets that.

I'm A One Woman Man . . . . **George Jones**

The song George would sing to his wife.

I Didn't See a Thing . . . . . . **George Jones & Ray Charles**

"I'm open and willing to record one with anybody that wants to." Recording with Ray Charles was one of George's favorite experiences.

Sing Me a Sad Song . . . . **Merle Haggard**
The song Merle was playing the day he and George met.

Choices . . . . **George Jones**
The song that sums up George's life.

How to Use This Book

Read this book in front of your computer while you search for downloadable music (legally, of course!). Whether you download whole playlists, only the songs that particularly interest you, or browse the thirty-second free clips that legal downloadable music sites provide, the volume in hand is a sourcebook that will allow you to enter the world of Country in a way never possible before the advent of the Internet and the rise of new technology. If at anytime you would like to see these lists individually, modify the lists, create your own favorite Country lists or purchase any of the songs/lists please visit our website at www.mycountryroots.com.

Very few people have ever owned three hundred albums, but now anyone who owns a computer has access to thousands upon thousands of songs—too many songs to navigate without guidance. In fact, this plethora of songs can be overwhelming, and so we go back to what we know again and again. Many mp3 players and iPods are as boring as FM radio; few are as interesting as the best independent radio station in town. This book is a solution to that problem.

Not only will we help you organize your music, we want to help you systematically explore, evaluate, critique, and develop an awareness of one of the most dynamic art forms of both the Gutenberg era and the cyberspace era: the song lyric.

We're starting with Country songs in this series. Country is America's ultimate outsider art. We've created a musical feast of Country songs for you to dip into. Newbies will find this an accessible introduction to the genre; aficionados will be inspired to name their candidates for songs that should have made the list, define other themes worthy of the list, shuffle the arrangement of songs on the lists, and evict songs from a list to install them on another. Shuffling is good. Together we will develop a Country canon, an understanding of the songs that we, today's listeners, feel are significant.

Our lists are idiosyncratic and provocative by design, not definitive. Each raises many questions: What is the connection between these songs? Is there a song that does not belong on the list? Is there a song that is clearly more successful artistically than the others on the list? What makes it so? Is there a song or songs on the list that fail? Is there a song you would like to add from another list in the book to this list? Is there a song not in the book that you would like to add? From the songs provided, what are the dimensions of the theme as you understand them? What are the connections of this theme in Country to other musical genres with which you are familiar? What song on the list goes

MY COUNTRY ROOTS

on your desert island playlist? Your "pick me up" list? Your "slow me down" list? Your "just barely making it" list? Your "exercise" list? Your "go to sleep" list? Pick. Shuffle.Create the playlists you want.

This volume you have in your hands is soon to be archaic. It is an artifact from an age associated with the printing of the *Gutenberg* Bible that began to end the day the very first civilian used the Internet. We're repurposing old technology to enhance the new. And we're using that new technology to show you an art form you don't know or will know now in a new way. Welcome to our roots: an idiosyncratic guide to Country music in cyberspace and your instrument for creating the unique playlists that will become the soundtrack to your life.

Who We Are

We are the icons who define what it means to be Country—or at least, the roles country folk are most likely to be playing when you find them at the center of a Country song. These cast-in-song-heroes and heroines represent aspects of what it means to be human that often go ignored for being too simple, too ugly, too ordinary, or too far beyond the law. You'll find yourself both comfortable and uncomfortable among the raggedy and righteous souls who populate the Country landscape.

1 Honky Tonk Angels

Offering an invitation into a world of intoxication, danger, and companionship, honky tonk angels inhabit and provide a way into a realm set apart from home, nature, or work (that is, unless you are a waitress). Partly victims, partly free agents, transcendent and transgressing, the women who frequent bars are powerful and alluring creatures of the night. Always female, the particular character of an individual honky tonk angel is often revealed by examining why she is in the bar, what she does while there, who she does it with, who she has left behind to do it, and who's watching while it all goes on.

It Wasn't God Who Made Honky Tonk Angels . . . . . Kitty Wells

Honky tonk angels are man-made.

Barroom Girls . . . . Gillian Welch

A Gillian Welch masterpiece, this song captures the ephemeral but real joys of being a barroom girl. From the opening metaphor that compares the night that falls apart to a dress that falls open, to the closing refrain that compares the jewelry and finery worn by young women to stars of the morning, the women described and the language used are divinely beautiful. After listening to this song, you may want a little smoke in your curls, too.

Rita Ballou. . . . . Guy Clark

With an exuberant "rawhide rope and velvet texture," Rita Ballou entrances and inspires the men of the Texas hill country.

Fist City . . . . Loretta Lynn

Honky tonk Angels battle each other and many a catfight begins in a honky tonk.

She's More to Be Pitied Than Scolded ..... The Seldom Scene

A patronizing apology, this song describes one woman's descent from honky tonk angel ingenue to a very different sub-genre of the genus, the aging honky tonk angel. This tired and overly painted cherubim attempts to hide a youth, which is fleeing faster than bad friends and too many nights of too much beer, too much wine, and too many parties.

Queen of the Silver Dollar .... Emmylou Harris

Her highness holds court at the local tavern, where jesters with drink in hand try to woo her to their bed. The song leaves open to interpretation whether or not these jesters have to "pay to play" (in silver dollars, of course). Written by Shel Silverstein.

'Cause Cheap is How I Feel .... Cowboy Junkies

Here we have an urban honky tonk angel in a big city bar, but the fear of the cold and the fear of poverty, almost as much as the steel guitar and delicate mandolin dancing across the track brushing against the brazen slide guitar, mark this honest expression of "you give what you get"—a country song. Though the intoxications are different and the dangers new, the pain of transgression and the promise of transcendence remain.

Wild Side of Life .... Wanda Jackson

A furious man writes his wife a letter accusing her of being—among other things—an "anybody's baby," who drinks in liquor and glamour instead of milk.

Pay No Attention to Alice .... Tom T. Hall

It doesn't sound like Alice is the only one who's drunk all the time. Where do you think the husband, army buddy, and wife, were off to when they ran the car into a ditch? We see through the haze of the grape to the farm girl charm that allows Alice to make apple pie and biscuits from recollection.

I'm A Honky Tonk Girl .... Loretta Lynn

An abandoned woman becomes a honky tonk prototype, craving drink and loud music, crying tears, ashamed of what she has become.

Honky Tonk Badonkadonk .... Trace Adkins

Honky tonk angels often look life-changingly good in tight britches.

You Ain't Woman Enough to Take My Man .... Tina Turner

A honky tonk declaration, written and made famous by the woman from Butcher Holler, Kentucky, is sung here by the woman from Nutbush, Tennessee

Honky Tonk Women.................. The Rolling Stones

The Stones testify that honky tonk angels, snatches of heaven on earth, are not bound by geographical or cultural borders. The singer encounters both the hard-partying ways of a Memphis "queen" and the contained refinement of a New York divorcee. Both take him for a whirl and leave him begging like a baby for more soul saving—even though he knows it's gonna hurt like hell in the morning. The sounds of Mississippi, Chicago, and London are wrapped together in a bar-shaking tune.

MY COUNTRY ROOTS

2 Honky Tonk Men

White southern men who revel and rebel in the part of life not defined by family, work, or God. Often found near honky tonk angels, these notably secular and universal characters are not to be confused with barroom devils.

Live Fast, Love Hard, Die Young. . . . .**Faron Young**

He doesn't need your approval. He tells grandiose lies, particularly to himself. He wants to satisfy a whole lot of women. He's a honky tonk man.

Guitars, Cadillacs. . . . . **Dwight Yoakam**

Honky tonk men have style.

**There's a Honky Tonk Angel
(Who'll Take Me Back In)** . . . . **Conway Twitty**

Honky tonk men have "other" women.

In the Jailhouse Now . . . .**Webb Pierce**

There is a very fine line that honky tonk men walk between drinking, shooting dice, picking up women...and going to jail. This is a Pierce classic.

Understand Your Man. . . . .**Johnny Cash**

Honky tonk men will leave you shamelessly.

Your Goddamn Mouth. . . . .**Freakwater**

He's got his tongue inside a beer bottle and God only knows where else, and he's glad she's there to call him out on it.

**Good Friends, Good Whiskey,
Good Loving**. . . . .**Hank Williams, Jr.**

The basic requirements for a good life are available at a honky tonk.

Back Up Buddy . . . .**Carl Smith**

Honky tonk men fight with each other often, particularly over women.

**All My Rowdy Friends
Are Coming Over Tonight**. . . . .**Hank Williams, Jr.**

Honky tonk behavior sometimes happens outside of the honky tonk.

Tryin' To Find Atlantis . . . . Jamie O'Neal

Trying to find a good man in a honky tonk or elsewhere is like trying to find a mythical city.

Only Daddy That'll Walk the Line . . . . Waylon Jennings

Some honky tonk men do right.

All My Rowdy Friends Have Settled Down . . Hank Williams, Jr.

Honky tonk days inevitably come to an end.

Honkytonk Man . . . . Marty Robbins

A honky tonk man invites a sad honky tonk angel to walk through the world with him after both have been cuckolded by their respective partners. Their minds set on mutual rescue, in the end they walk out of the honky tonk with the best gifts it can possibly offer: love, music, and no pain, be it for a night or forever.

MY COUNTRY ROOTS

3 | Good Women

Good women love well. They are committed, loyal, passionate, and patient. They are clear and uncomplicated compensations living complex lives.

Good Hearted Woman ...... Waylon Jennings & Willie Nelson

There's a certain naiveté in the confidence expressed by the "good timin' man" that sings this Country classic. Is she really that patient with him or is that what she wants him to think?

When I Think about Cheating .... Gretchen Wilson

Leave it to a woman to think about it—and really think about it hard—before deciding that her current love isn't worth jeopardizing. There is a moral here, folks.

Pearl, Pearl, Pearl .... Flatt & Scruggs

Flatt & Scruggs vie for the love of one, Pearl, in this simple bluegrass number. Note the strength and power of Scruggs's banjo playing.

My Elusive Dreams .... Tammy Wynette and David Houston

A husband and wife move from city to city looking for the work and dreams that continue to slip through their fingers. In the end, they find that all they have is each other. Thank goodness.

Good Woman's Love .... Tony Rice

He could have become a drifter, a drinker, a loner, and a goner if it weren't for a good woman and her capacity to hold his heart and steer him in the direction only she can.

Ruby Ann .... Marty Robbins

Somewhere between the honky tonk sound and the Buddy Holly sock-hop sensibility lives this song about a woman who could have money and riches, but instead chooses the poor man she loves.

That's the Way Love Goes .... Johnny Rodriguez

A sweet love letter to the power of love to triumph over the pitfalls and travails of life by Country music's first Mexican-born star. Other recordings of note: Merle Haggard and Lefty Frizzell.

Sunday Kind of Woman ....Charlie Rich

For the man who has a tendency to wake up in beds not his own, there is always a moment of clarity when a good wholesome woman seems to be the remedy. If only he could be so lucky.

My Arms Stay Open Late ....Tammy Wynette

This song describes a tragically good woman, one who knows, acknowledges, and yet condones her man's cheating ways. Loyalty is loyalty, even if it is not reciprocated.

Van Lear Rose............................Loretta Lynn

In this biographical sketch, Lynn tells the story of a Kentucky beauty who chooses the heart of the poor boy over her other cocky suitors.

Nellie Kane ....Hot Rize

A rambling man quits his travelin' ways when he meets the love of his life and her son in North Dakota. Though Hot Rize was only together for a brief period in the 1980s, they remain one of the great bands within the bluegrass genre.

How Mountain Girls Can Love ....The Stanley Brothers

A bluegrass standard, this ode to the women of the Blue Ridge Mountains runs fast and furious, paced by a banjo and tight brotherly harmonies. The song possibly refers to the hills of Roane County Virginia where the Stanley Brothers grew up.

MY COUNTRY ROOTS

4 | Ramblers

These descendents of the adventurous Huckleberry Finn and Natty Bumpo light out to see new territory even as it vanishes. Honoring the wild promise of America as an inviting wilderness to be explored, these characters complicate the lives of the people to whom they are attached while retaining their own ironic simplicity.

Rake and Rambling Man . . . . Don Williams

Love and a good woman are truly the only things that can make a wandering man settle down.

I'm a Rambling Man . . . . Waylon Jennings

A catchy, telecaster-guitar driven shuffle, this song serves as a warning to unsuspecting honky tonk angels about the pitfalls of fooling around with those who make a living rambling.

Leaving Louisiana in the Broad Daylight . . . . . Rodney Crowell

This is the story of a girl who falls for a rambler and the unfortunate ending that ensues down on the bayou. Other recordings of note: Emmylou Harris and the Oak Ridge Boys.

I Am a Pilgrim . . . . Doc Watson

This religious rambler is a pilgrim who wanders in search of a land beyond the skies. A mountain gospel standard, this song has been recorded by countless Country artists.

Don't Fence Me In . . . . Gene Autry

The famous Cole Porter cowboy ode to solitude and independence, originally written for the 1944 movie *Hollywood Canteen*.

I've Been Everywhere . . . . Hank Snow

One of the most fun songs of the genre it features the acrobatic delivery of a lyric that lists nearly one hundred towns in a little over two minutes. Snow's baritone articulation is without rival.

I'm a Long Gone Daddy . . . . Hank Williams

Recorded in 1949, too much nagging, pouting, and moaning sends a long, tall daddy out the door to ride the rails.

Wayfaring Stranger ....**Johnny Cash**

Recorded by everyone from Burl Ives to Bill Monroe to Emmylou Harris, this somber song is most honest in this Cash recording. Simple, stark, and spiritually hopeful.

Rambling Man.....................**The Allman Brothers**

The band's signature anthem defines the archetype of the 1970s southern rock-and-roll musician. Listening to this just makes you want to get on the highway—right now!

Hello, I'm Gone ....**Trisha Yearwood**

A woman realizes that leaving is the only thing she has left and she couldn't be happier about it. This is an intimate, soulful track with a catchy chorus. Written by revered, but under-recognized songwriter, Kevin Welch.

Ramble On Rose ....**The Grateful Dead**

Vintage Jerry Garcia guitar dominates this mid-tempo masterpiece about the wicked, wild, and mythic Rose. This is psychedelic Country at its best.

A Rude and Rambling Man.......**Jody Stecher & Kate Brislin**

A rambler chooses to settle down and marry, and ends up in jail as a result. Mandolin/guitar interplay and tight harmonies move this song right out the door.

Along about Daybreak ....**The Bluegrass Album Band**

This is a "goodbye letter" of sorts from a husband to his wife and children, featuring a characteristic high-tenor vocal and an all-star bluegrass lineup.

Freeborn Man ....**Junior Brown**

Brown's striking bass/baritone vocals interplay with his virtuosic and bawdy steel guitar on this song about a rambling man, whom most are happier to see leaving than arriving.

He Went to Paris........................**Jimmy Buffett**

An aging international drifter looks back on a life in an honest and, ultimately, grateful way.

5 Outlaws/Bandits

They are ramblers with a purpose and a motive. Sometimes criminal, at their most significant, they are committed to ideal purposes not supported by the majority. These men are willing to endure wrath and punishment to maintain integrity and freedom. Outlaws and bandits are of special importance to poor Southerners, both white and black, who share very different, but somehow common historical experiences of having the law against them.

Pancho and Lefty . . . . **Willie Nelson & Merle Haggard**

The archetypical "partners in crime" song about an unlikely duo. Pancho loses his life and Lefty loses his soul. The listener is left to decide which is worse. This one also appears on the Friends list.

Pretty Boy Floyd . . . . **Woody Guthrie**

A story of an Oklahoma outlaw, a Robin Hood of sorts, who is hung for the killing of a deputy, the song is a social commentary on the unjust punishment of good people. Note the similarity in language and subject to Bob Marley's reggae classic "I Shot the Sheriff" and Eric Clapton's subsequent cover of the same song, in which he poignantly claims he did not shoot the deputy.

Ballad of Spider John . . . . **Jimmy Buffett**

Written by Willis Allan Ramsey, this is a beautiful tale of a broken-hearted old thief who humbly recalls how gambling, booze, and robbery forced him down the road of solitude and alienation.

Been All Around This World . . . . **David Grisman & Jerry Garcia**

This is a song of traditional origin, which utilizes the call-and-response lyric, about an outlaw in the Blue Ridge Mountains.

Wanted Man . . . . **Johnny Cash**

Being a fugitive in one state is bad, but being a fugitive everywhere is outlaw. A dark shadow of Hank Snow's "I've Been Everywhere."

Midnight Rider . . . . **The Allman Brothers**

A high school, southern-rock anthem, the song explores the existential outlaw in all of us and reminds us that the art of being an outlaw is thinking you can't be caught.

Real Mean Bottle .... Vince Gill

An ode to Merle Haggard, Country music's most famous graduate of the notorious San Quentin Prison. Was it the booze that made him do it?

Outlaws Like Us .... Travis Tritt

This tribute to Country music's renegades asks and answers the question, "Are the songwriting outlaws alive and well?"

Ain't No God in Mexico .... Waylon Jennings

Life in a Mexican prison will make any American outlaw think twice about breaking the law in a strange land.

The Road Goes On Forever............... Robert Earl Keen

A modern Bonnie and Clyde tale that you might find on a tabloid cover at the supermarket. But in this song, Bonnie walks off into the sunset.

6 Bad Mamas

These are affecting tales—not of women who do their men wrong, but of women who do their children, most often daughters, wrong.

Lucille . . . . **Kenny Rogers**

Over a tumbler of whiskey in an Ohio bar, a man falls in and then out of lust for lady who left her husband and kids at home. Having the conversation interrupted by her husband killed their flirtatious liaison.

The Sun Was Blood Red And Going Down. . . . . . **Tanya Tucker**

One of the darkest songs in Country music, this is a story of a man and his daughter on the hunt for mommy. They find her at a tavern with another man. Believe it or not, it gets even worse.

Mama Loved Men . . . . **Garth Brooks**

Daddy's off earning money. Mama's off cheating. Daddy commits double homicide with a truck. Kids are left with a dead mother and an incarcerated father.

What's Your Mama's Name Child . . . . **Tanya Tucker**

Mama has been keeping a secret from her green-eyed girl for a long time now. It's about time she explored the city of New Orleans and someone named Buford Wilson.

Pistol-Packin' Mama . . . . **Jimmie Rodgers**

You might want to think about messin' with a Pistol Packin' Mama. The person you're foolin' around with might want to think about it too.

Everything that Glitters Is Not Gold . . . . **Dan Seals**

Mama leaves her family in pursuit of fame and glory on the rodeo circuit. She doesn't even call on her daughter's birthday. She's a bad mama, but her daughter has a great daddy. Another Bob McDill classic.

The Man that Turned My Mama On. . . . . **Tanya Tucker**

A wholesome girl taught to follow her mother's example runs away with a musician. A generation later, that wholesome girl's daughter wonders who her daddy is.

Bedtime Story . . . . **Tammy Wynette**

Both curious and disturbing, a mother tucks her daughter into bed and decides to lull her to sleep with the story of how her daddy cheated on her mommy.

Mama Tried . . . . **Merle Haggard**

"I turned twenty-one in prison doing life without parole." What can we say? Mama tried, and failed.

Birmingham Mistake . . . .**Sammi Smith**

An abandoned infant turns into a depressed woman with more passion for the mother who abandoned her than for living her own life. Thanks to mama, it's a short trip from the orphan's basket to the suicide casket.

Fancy . . . . **Reba McEntire**

Mom, sick and without a husband, sends Fancy out to turn tricks for the family dollar. A tale of stark survival and a story of a streetwalker who goes from rags-to-riches. Written and originally performed by Bobbie Gentry.

7 Hookers

These are the female outlaws and bandits of the Country canon. They too break the rules for a reason, be it poverty and survival or fury and compassion. Often ironic, and almost always subversive, these characters challenge our understanding of love, money, and virtue.

The Son of Hickory Hollow's Tramp . . .The Country Gentlemen

More than a vice, prostitution is a business. It provides a service for a fee, and in more cases than we might believe, that fee supports a family. Prostitutes can be good moms, too. A traditional bluegrass arrangement.

Tecumseh Valley. . . . . Townes Van Zandt

A girl by the name of Caroline wanders into a town, starts turning tricks for Gypsy Sally, and ends up on the wrong side of fare thee well.

My Bucket's Got a Hole in It . . . . Hank Williams

A complex song, one has to wonder if it's about poverty or prostitution. Just how did he get that Ford?

The Bargain Store. . . . . Dolly Parton

An invitation from soft-spoken madam who, despite her age, can still give you what you need.

Let Him Roll. . . . . Guy Clark

For one man, heaven was a prostitute in Dallas. That is until he asked her to be his wife. A ballad so honest, it should come with a tissue.

Helen Of Troy, Pennsylvania . . . . .Darrell Scott

Twin banjos in unison sweep you into a story of awkward excitement about two adolescent boys who engage the services of a prostitute more than twice their age.

Rhonda's Last Ride . . . . .Darrell Scott

A toast from one man, down on his luck, to a woman who wasn't as lucky.

If I Lose . . . . .J.E. Mainer

This bluegrass number proclaims that any negative outcome that may arise from paying for love is well worth the brief moment of ecstasy.

Sally Was a Good Old Girl . . . . **Waylon Jennings**

Yeah, Sally was a good ole girl, but was it because she did what you wanted and gave you what you needed? Just what kind of work did Sally do? Even if money was exchanged, it seems that it was done in a heartfelt way.

Three Wooden Crosses. . . . . **Randy Travis**

A hooker, a bus accident, a blood-stained Bible, and a second chance are just a few of the elements in this mystery of inspiration.

MY COUNTRY ROOTS

8 | Rednecks

"The 'R' word" has everything to do with laboring, poor, white, southern identity. A persona that is either a source of pride or humiliation, the redneck is a character that says much about the convergence of issues of class, caste, and race in the South. Often used humorously, and sometimes proudly, the phrase can impart a load of pain. Different from a blue-collar factory worker, a redneck is an outdoor laborer. Contrasted against white-collar life, the title signifies poor, white people in a wide variety of job categories and geographies.

Redneck Woman . . . . **Gretchen Wilson**

She's not an idea, she's a reality. And she knows the plural of y'all is "all y'all."

Redneck Girl . . . .**The Kentucky Headhunters**

She's cruising in her daddy's pickup, and she doesn't yet have a baby on her hip, but she's on her way to having one and this redneck boy wants to go with her.

Redneck Romeo . . . . **Confederate Rodeo**

He wears Old Spice, drinks Falstaff beer, owns 27 ball caps, and spends his whole paycheck buying drinks and playing the jukebox. He is self-deceived and deceiving, an ever-present staple in honky tonks.

Redneck Yacht Club. . . . . **Craig Morgan**

Sounds better than the regular yacht club. "Let's go to the lake," is a well-known redneck mating call. Picture a trailer park on water.

Rednecks, White Socks,
   and Blue Ribbon Beer. . . . .**Johnny Russell**

All the people and things that decorate the most comfortable country bars.

Uneasy Rider. . . . .**The Charlie Daniels Band**

Long hair gets a white boy in trouble in the honky tonk, but his intimate knowledge of white southern bias gets him out. This song displays the edge of the hippy-country boy conflict. Rednecks can be dangerous, too.

Up Against the Wall Redneck Mother . . . . . .**Jerry Jeff Walker**

Mr. Walker calls the mothers of rednecks to account. What's all this about Falstaff Beer? Another edge of the hippy-country boy conflict.

Again rednecks can be dangerous. This could also fit in the Bad Mamas list.

Night of the Living Rednecks . . . . The Dead Kennedys

Belligerent, antagonistic, an anti-Country song. But the anti-wealth bias is Country. And there is a Country guitar groove going on beneath the lead singer's shout that gives precedence to Kentucky Fried chicken over McDonalds McNuggets.

Long Haired Redneck 2001 . . . . David Allan Coe

"My long hair can't cover up my redneck." If you are willing to fight, and whisper, and sing the songs about Texas, and know every song that Hank Williams ever wrote, you may look like a hippy, but you have exquisite Country credentials.

Your Redneck Past . . . . Ben Folds Five

Something you might want to hide. This song doesn't sound redneck, but it reflects the existence of rednecks that can pass for WASP (White Anglo-Saxon Protestant of the richer persuasion)!

Red Neckin' Love Makin' Night . . . . Conway Twitty

Then again, you could just celebrate your redneck present. This man knows who he is and what he wants.

Red Clay Halo . . . . Gillian Welch

Red dirt stains things. Some white people colored by labor, earth and poverty, might more meaningfully be considered red. Is the stain gone when they arrive in heaven? Is it changed to a crowning halo?

MY COUNTRY ROOTS

9 Angels

Country angels are vulnerable, ethereal, worthy, women, ambassadors of heaven walking on earth. These songs mix hope, and longing, tragedy and transcendence.

Angel from Montgomery .Bonnie Raitt

One of the most beautiful Country songs of all time, written by John Prine. An old woman looks back at her life and forward to her future. Either way life is hard, unless you're an escaping angel, a woman who manages to rise above the South's silent men and mythic images as she gives color and flavor to real life.

Angel Flying Too Close to the Ground . . . . Willie Nelson

A lover, struggling with demons, is injured. When she is healed, she leaves the love that soothed her. Some would judge her ungrateful, but Willie doesn't. He simply promises to remember. So will we all.

Infamous Angel. . . . . .Iris Dement

A young girl sows her wild oats and is welcomed back to a home that appreciates the adventures she has undertaken.

Misguided Angel. . . . . .Cowboy Junkies

Is it her, or is it him that she compares to Gabriel and Lucifer? A young woman defends the man she loves from her family, even as she recognizes her family in the man she loves. Misguided angels all, we seem to return to that which confounds us.

Lake Charles . . . . .Lucinda Williams

A complex friend has a complex death. The question at the center of the song haunts like a wish. We can only hope an angel was present and spoke the words Lucinda imagined.

Play Me the Waltz of the Angels . . . . The Derailers

An old man requests the band play the song that was playing the night he met his wife and the day he buried her.

Angel Band . . . . .The Stanley Brothers

Traditional, shining, white-robed angels circle round, then swing over the river Jordan carrying those washed in the blood to victory in Jesus.

Ten Thousand Angels . . . . Mindy McCready

She needs ten thousand angels to help her say *no*.

Lo-fi Tennessee Mountain Angel . . . . **Whiskeytown**

This angel plays in a punk rock band. She is a high-winged irony and enigma.

Angel of the Morning . . . . **Juice Newton**

This angel conveniently flies away in the morning. She's who the man was looking for in Glen Campbell's, "Gentle on My Mind."

Kiss an Angel Good Morning . . . . **Charley Pride**

A man and a woman in love. It's enough to make this man start thinking about angels.

Return of the Grievous Angel . . . . **Gram Parsons**

Twenty thousand roads lead the grievous angel to return home to a certain calico bonnet. Did the cowboy angels assist him in his return or impede his journey? Was he able to unbuckle that old Bible belt? A seminal influence on every love and travel song in Country music thereafter, this song also has a home on the Rambler list.

MY COUNTRY ROOTS

10 Black

The influence of Africa on the sound of Country music is present in every banjo strum and blue yodel recorded in Country. The black street musician Rufus "Tee Tot" Payne is thought by many to be Hank Williams's most significant early influence, and a black man by the name of Arnold Schultz is cited by Bill Monroe as an early mentor. Africa is present in both the instrumentation of bluegrass bands and in the way bluegrass bands swap instrumental leads in a fashion related to that of jazz players that contrasts starkly with the playing style of old-time musicians. Unfortunately the African-American experience in the South and the Southerner's observations of that experience are far less evident. The songs that follow are notable exceptions.

Old Dogs, Children, and Watermelon Wine . . . . Tom T. Hall

It is a conversation between an old, black gentleman and a songwriter at an airport. The songwriter appraises the janitor's life conclusions; the janitor picks up the younger man's change. Wonder if our fictional janitor thought he was robbed when he heard the song on the lounge radio? Maybe he was proud?

Get Rhythm . . . . Johnny Cash

A shoeshine boy gives his advice and a grown man listens. Racist, racialist, or race appreciating? You decide. Maybe the grinning "boy" hides something worth knowing in his mask as well as well as behind his mask.

Johnny B. Goode . . . . Chuck Berry

Black competence, pure and simple.

The Yellow Rose of Texas . . . . Jimmy Wakely

For six weeks in 1955, this was the number one song in the nation. Earlier versions of this song claimed, "she's the sweetest rose of color a fellow ever knew," giving rise to the suspicion that the girl celebrated in this song was a beautiful mulatto woman. Some say the banjo that the lovers play in the song signifies this.

Let's Jump the Broomstick . . . . Brenda Lee

Little Miss Dynamite is making a very interesting invitation. Jumping the broomstick is a ritual act that enslaved Africans performed to marry themselves. Today, it persists as an African-American wedding custom.

There's a Little Bit of Hank in Me . . . . **Charley Pride**

Here, Charley acknowledges the influence of Hank Williams, Sr. Williams himself, as noted above, was influenced by black bluesman Rufus Payne, better known as "Tee Tot," who was seldom publicly acknowledged by Hank Williams.

Hey, Porter . . . . **Johnny Cash**

We know little about the porter in this song. His thoughts about crossing beneath the Mason-Dixon line go unnoticed. The porter is presented as an aide-memoir, a part of the South that travels, like the smell of frost on cotton leaves.

Mr. Bojangles . . . . **Jerry Jeff Walker**

An ode to a black man who travels through Dixie, dancing for handouts while mourning a dead dog. Bojangles is a performer at once liberated and trapped by his performance. This song could also be on a number of lists: Honky Tonkin', Jails & Prisons, Alcohol, and Crazy.

Catfish John . . . . **Jerry Garcia**

A formerly enslaved river hobo is claimed as kin. As opposed to Cash's grinning while laboring Negro in "Get Rhythm," Bob McDill and Alan Reynolds simply acknowledge that the dark gentleman's load was hard to bear." No apologies, no explanations, just stone Country truth. A quiet masterpiece.

Ruben James. . . . . **Kenny Rogers**

A white boy is raised well by a black sharecropper. The song expresses pure, unadulterated love. Some folks know how to say "thank you."

The Ballad of Sally Anne . . . . **Mark O'Connor**

Between his wedding and his reception, a man is lynched. His bride, Sally Ann asks, first in life, then as a ghost, "Whose gonna dance with Sally Ann?" Who will accept responsibility for this violent act? This song is usually rendered as an instrumental John Cowan sings.

11 John Henry

The most famous black person in Country music is also the most famous laborer in Country music. Some consider the ultimate theme of all the John Henry songs to be the destruction of man by machines. Others consider the central theme of the John Henry songs to be the triumph of will over technology, character over plot, and soul over event.

John Henry . . . . Big Boy Henry

He was the black man who bested the machine and died. This John Henry, a steel driving man, wields a fifteen-pound hammer. The song asserts that Polly's loving in the night sustains John Henry's work in the day. It also slyly equates John Henry's driving and pounding during the day with his love making at night. On his deathbed, Polly Ann exclaims, "John Henry I'm deep in love with you. Ain't gonna have no other man."

Patches . . . . Clarence Carter

A boy does the work of a man.

John Henry . . . . Leadbelly

In this version, John Henry lies in state at the White House upon his death, and all the passing locomotives pay him homage. This version adds the idea that "Polly drove steel like a man."

John Henry . . . . Bill Monroe

This up-tempo version begins with a tiny John Henry standing in someone's hand. This song is more about the work of picking and singing than about steel driving.

The Legend of John Henry's Hammer . . . . Johnny Cash

There is superb storytelling in this epic, nearly nine-minute long version of the Johnny Henry tale. Cash weaves multiple thematic strands throughout the song, including the man versus machine story, the racial conflict, and the sex sustaining labor theme to name three. Cash extends the frame of the story, adding the history of John Henry's childhood: John Henry inherits his hammer from his father, who leaves it to him just before being carried off to jail. The delicious details make this the best of Country John Henry songs. From "John Henry's mammy had about a dozen babies, John Henry's Daddy broke jail about a dozen times," to the sly, "yeah, that was his *good* woman," insinuating other women in John Henry's life, to the essential moment when John Henry dies and Polly Ann takes his place to show just who she is and who he was, this is the unforgettable tale of John Henry, a steel driving man.

Molly and the Tenbrooks . . . . .Bill Monroe

Tenbrooks, a racehorse, runs fast enough to beat the Memphis train, but the need for its labor ends, as industry eclipses flesh and blood effort. Some believe Monroe's earliest version to be the first true recording/ instrumentation of what later became known as bluegrass music.

Spike Driver Blues . . . . Mississippi John Hurt

A country blues version of the John Henry song. A black man rejects his hammer, the hammer that killed John Henry, claiming that he won't let it kill him.

Mariano . . . . Robert Earl Keen

A variation of the John Henry story starring a Mexican migrant worker. The man of the house watches, across a divide of culture and race, an honest laborer straining to support his family.

MY COUNTRY ROOTS

12 Teen Girls

What it takes to get a girl to leave home and what it will take for her to grow to be the kind of woman who will one day make a home she will not leave—that's what these songs are all about.

Strawberry Wine .... Deana Carter

A seventeen-year old girl loses her virginity with a college boy working on her grandparents' farm.

Ballad of a Teenage Queen .... June Carter Cash

The girl next door gets discovered by Hollywood, becomes a big star, but gives it all up for the boy next door.

The Wings Upon Your Horns .... Loretta Lynn

This song, about the loss of teenage virginity, is one of many songs of Lynn's that was banned by Country music radio.

Suds in the Bucket .... Sara Evans

A good little girl turns into a spunky young woman while no one is looking. Halfway through her chores she runs off with a boy, leaving the whole town talking.

Walk Away Joe .... Trisha Yearwood

A mother warns her daughter to take it slow, but the daughter runs off with a young man who leaves her waiting in the car while he robs a Texaco. And then leaves her while she is sleeping. The phrase, "wrong kind of paradise" was coined here.

John Deere Green .... Joe Diffie

Billy Bob paints his name, Charlene's name, and a three-foot heart in green paint smack-dab in the middle of town. The whole town thinks he should have used red, but Charlene has a farmer fetish.

She's in Love with the Boy .... Trisha Yearwood

A girl comes home later than she's supposed to, and Daddy is mad. Her Mama reminds her Daddy that once upon a time her own father thought he was a bad idea, too.

Wake Up Little Susie .... The Everly Brothers

Susie's waking up from the dream of childhood, into the life of a passionate young woman who falls asleep in her boyfriend's arms—

after the two have been doing who knows what. But we know what her parents suspect they've been doing.

T-R-O-U-B-L-E .... Travis Tritt

Pretty mamas have pretty babies, and pretty babies one day turn into pretty mamas. Originally recorded by Elvis Presley.

Orphan Girl .... Gillian Welch

She's got friends and she's got God. She's on her way. This orphan girl is far more Miss Independence than Miss Self-Pity. True country pride takes root at an early age and in both sexes.

44 Stories .... Roseanne Cash

An intimate portrait of the textures of intimate conversations between mothers and daughters as the daughters become women.

Little Queenie .... Chuck Berry

Being a teenage girl is about finding your beauty just as the world is finding it too.

Little Sister .... Dwight Yoakam

There comes a time when a girl's face and body change rapidly, and for the better. There also comes an awareness in a boy's life that sometimes girls want to kiss one fellow and then another. But there's always hope that a sweet young girl won't grow that particular bad habit.

13 Feminists

Quietly and surely, feminists have a secure home in Country music. Birth control, abortion, fair wage for females, and cultural oppression have all been topics of immensely popular Country radio standards.

9 to 5 . . . . **Dolly Parton**

This song is a countrypolitan lament. Women who escape the jail of pregnancy begin to discover the prison of the office place.

The Pill . . . . **Loretta Lynn**

Staking a claim on sexuality without babies, Lynn renegotiates the terms of marital freedom.

XXX's and OOO's . . . . **Trisha Yearwood**

A woman struggles to follow in both her father's and her mother's footsteps at the same time.

Harper Valley PTA . . . . **Jeannie C. Riley**

A young widowed wife ridicules her fellow citizens' hypocrisy. Her young daughter cheers as her Mama refuses to be stigmatized by her status as an unmarried woman with sexual experience.

Rated X . . . . **Loretta Lynn**

When virginity truly mattered, a divorced young woman was significantly marked for having already been married. The young divorcee is sexually experienced, dangerous, and vulnerable.

Coward of the County . . . . **Kenny Rogers**

A gang-raped young woman is cherished and avenged by her husband.

Red Rag Top . . . . **Tim McGraw**

After an abortion, the girl stops loving the boy.

I Wish I Was a Single Girl . . . . **Rose Maddox and the Maddox Brothers**

"Yonder he comes with a bottle in his hand, wishing I was dead and he had another dram." In this song, marriage is a hellhole, which is a prototypical feminist sentiment. This song was recorded as early as 1925.

Working Girl Blues. . . . . .Hazel Dickens

It has been reported that Dickens wrote this song on the back of an inventory slip. With Marxist insight and a Country twang, this working girl knows someone is profiting from her prison of poverty. She makes a claim on freedom and beauty with her white blue yodel.

14 Ladies of Legend

They are the stars of the Country canon. Vividly drawn portraits of unforgettable women challenge patriarchal notions that good women should remain invisible.

Jolene . . . . Dolly Parton

Quintessential Dolly. Jolene, the girl who has it all, wants *your* man—and has what it takes to get him. But is there more going on here than what is on the surface? Perhaps the narrator is using the potential love-theft of the man as an excuse to flatter and flirt with the woman?

Amanda . . . . Don Williams

An ode to a lady who stays committed to a man, who is committed to the life of an itinerate gypsy—the life of a performing musician. A song for everyone who chooses true love over ease, and genius over social class. Another Bob McDill classic.

Maybelline. . . . . Carl Perkins

Originally titled "Ida Red," by Chuck Berry (who based his version on an earlier song also called "Ida Red." The earlier song told the story of a slave woman who waits for her mistress to die, hoping she will inherit the freedom the mistress promised to leave her in her will. As rewritten by Berry and recorded by Carl Perkins, Maybelline is committed to erotic freedom rather than political freedom. Both incarnations of this song affirm a simple Country truth: *people are going to be who they are.*

Delta Dawn . . . . Tanya Tucker

Morning comes to a place and a person that once were beautiful in this Tucker classic. Southern patriarchy cannot protect the South or her daughters from the ravaging disinterest of new times and new men. In the wake of this transition, Delta Dawn is left to seek the shelter of insanity.

My Maria . . . . Brooks & Dunn

Here, the *other woman*—a gypsy woman—liberates a square man's soul, chasing away the blues that won't let this idealistic rambler alone. On the other hand, he's got some moral vision problems, but Maria cures those as well. Something says he will be back.

Elvira . . . . .The Oak Ridge Boys

Elvira is an intoxicating and infectious mix of sex and God. Her fiery presence reduces this grown boy to baby-talking, giving listeners some of the most explicit—or the silliest—lyrics in Country music. Elvira reminds us that when you've got good sex and a good God, you've got everything—even if you don't got money. Other recordings of note: Rodney Crowell.

Corrina, Corrina . . . . Mississippi John Hurt

She's a sexual adventuress who has both a lover and a true loving man. Hurt delivers the true loving man's perspective in this blues standard. The man in the story sounds like he's screaming at the bottom of the mountain.

Young Widow Brown . . . . Waylon Jennings

She's put one man in the grave and she's not afraid to drop another. This chick wants sex and money. He just wants to leave, but his heart won't let him.

Polk Salad Annie . . . . Tony Joe White

Her mother's in prison, her grandmother got ate by alligators, her daddy's lazy, and her brothers are thieves. Still, this resourceful young Southerner makes her own way in the world. Tony Joe White paints a legend with a combination of swamp-country imagery and a funked up Country stew.

I'm Not Lisa . . . . Jessi Colter

Sometimes a lady of legend is a problem for her less legendary competition. Julie is being called "Lisa" because Lisa is still on his mind. Pain is rarely so beautiful. An exquisite performance.

Ruby (Are You Mad at Your Man) . . . . The Osborne Brothers

This song about a miner's lady moves with the speed of a bullet and boasts one of the longest high tenor notes in bluegrass music when performed live.

Ruby, Don't Take Your Love to Town . . . . Kenny Rogers

A sexually deprived young woman leaves her wheelchair-bound war-vet lover to find the pleasure she desperately craves and deserves. *Lady Chatterley's Lover* in two minutes and fifty-four seconds, except that this vet has more compassion for his lady.

15 Mythic Men

This is a list dedicated to the men of myth, those creatures, both real and imagined, who have attained a level of legend through their surreally biographical songs.

Kaw-Liga . . . . Hank Williams

Hank mythologizes the wooden Indian that greeted customers at the front of general stores. He creates a tragic story of unrequited love between the Cigar Store Indian and a female wooden statue. The Apollo and Daphne of Country.

Ginseng Sullivan . . . . Norman Blake

A timeless lyric and wonderful portrait of a displaced man living in the mountains of North Georgia who hunts ginseng root. The irony, of course, is that Sullivan would make a killing on the top dollar root today.

Cotton Eyed Joe . . . . The Freight Hoppers

A ripping version of the traditional fiddle tune brought to you by this incredible old-time band from North Carolina. Legend has it that Joe was the best dancer folks had ever seen, and this tune summons his flat-footing spirit.

Fiddlin' Bill . . . . The Nashville Bluegrass Band

This song, about an old-time time fiddler who immortalizes himself through the fiddle tunes he keeps alive, features the unrivaled string-sawing of the great Stuart Duncan.

Uncle Pen . . . . Bill Monroe

A really good band has two fiddlers, a la Bob Wills. This tune was written by Monroe about his Uncle Pendleton Vandiver, who had a huge influence on his young nephew.

Daddy Sang Bass . . . . Johnny Cash

To most folks, daddy is the ultimate Mythic Man. Cash incorporates the song, "Will the Circle Be Unbroken" into this homage to family, unity, and melody.

Big John . . . . Tex Williams

This song, about a larger-than-life miner who died saving others in a mining tragedy, is the quintessential tall tale that moves from town to town and generation to generation, growing bigger with each telling.

Lazy John . . . . Brad Leftwich & Linda Higginbothem

A little-known tune preserved in recording by the great old-time fiddler, Brad Leftwich, this lyric speaks of an affable, hard-farming fella who works all week in anticipation of the big-time Saturday night dance. There's one in every town.

Casey Jones . . . . The Grateful Dead

Heading southbound on the Illinois Central from Memphis to New Orleans, Casey Jones ran headlong into another train heading northbound. He was killed and instantly became a folk hero. Many believe that Jones saved lives by staying at the controls and trying to slow the train down instead of bailing out, though it meant losing his own life.

MY COUNTRY ROOTS

16 Fools

Perhaps not so foolish after all, these characters comprise an interesting collection of Country anti-heroes. Humble yet subversive, they invite us to question the integrity and significance of the existing order. In many of these tunes shame gives way to pride—just at the point of loss.

Mr. Fool . . . . George Jones

Part of being a fool is pledging you will never be a fool again. This song finds Jones at his best vocally. With a tone sweeter than a fiddle, he kicks the hell out of this track.

Statue of a Fool . . . . Jack Greene

Who wouldn't want a statue of themselves? This cut imagines a statue of a fool in the center of town where men could come and see the idol of love's shame—deceived time and again.

Waltzing Fool . . . . Lyle Lovett

There are few things sadder than dancing alone. In this tune, love makes life's dance a solitary waltz for this fool.

Nobody But a Fool . . . . Connie Smith

The steady walk in this bouncy bass line pushes this woman confidently on down the road. When she reminds her beloved man that only an idiot could love him, she shames herself.

New Fool . . . . Alison Krauss

He may have won this time, but at some point his games won't play anymore—one day, when he falls in love and is left behind, he'll know what it's like to play the fool.

Fool #1 . . . . The Mavericks

Revisiting the Nashville sound developed by Owen Bradley and Chet Atkins in the 1950s, Raul Malo and The Mavericks depict a fool who knows he should leave, but just can't find a way to wake up and walk out.

Queen of Hearts . . . . Juice Newton

A big-time crossover Country hit in 1981, this tune expresses the foolish feelings of shame and embarrassment through the metaphor of gambling. Even if you don't like the twang, the syncopated lyric and pulsing guitar make this tune irresistible.

Now and Then There's a Fool Such As I . . . . Hank Snow

Not your garden variety fool, this fella regards himself as exceptionally ignorant in the ways of love.

The Women Make a Fool Out of Me . . . . .Ernest Tubb

Sometimes you feel like everything you do is wrong, and in the case of love, this guy can't stop striking out. He's got some serious problems.

100% Pure Fool . . . . The Derailers

Fueled by the combustible sound of telecaster guitar and pedal steel, this full-fledged fool sounds like he's been riding a runaway big-rig down a one-way track of regret.

Hey Crazy Fool . . . . Jerry Engler

A buddy gives a buddy advice: the one who makes a fool out of someone is the ultimate fool. A diamond in the rough, Jerry Engler, in a wobbly, soulful moan, warns his friend to stop using and abusing the woman he calls his own.

I'm Sorry . . . . Brenda Lee

It's difficult to tell exactly who she's apologizing to. The deep shame expressed in her repeated apologies leads us to believe that she's really not apologizing at all, but saying how pitiful she is.

Life of a Fool. . . . . Paul Burch

The fool in this song is just plain reckless, writing the story of his own demise and trying to take his friends down with him, too—but the singer/narrator fires a shot across his bow as a warning: Wake up dummy!

My Ears Should Burn When Fools
Are Talked About . . . . Claude Gray

How could he be so dumb as to waste something so good? It's all his fault, and his anger, self-loathing, and regret are apparent in this swinging lament for having cheated.

Same Fool . . . . Dwight Yoakam

This fool's had it up to here with being fooled, and he's not going to be fooled again—at least not the same way. Oh, woe is the fool.

Solid Gold Plated Fool . . . . Delbert McClinton

In this undeniably funky Country song, you start swinging with the spicy attitude McClinton shakes his woman's way—he may have been a real pushover up 'til now, but things are gonna change, or he's strutting away.

MY COUNTRY ROOTS

17 Mamas and Daddies

These songs have a felt reverential quality. Songs that celebrate mamas and daddies doing their jobs well often come perilously close to idolatry.

Drive (For Daddy Gene) . . . . **Alan Jackson**
A daddy teaches a child to use and enjoy freedom, knowing that the best teachers can expect to be left behind. Ain't a mama in sight.

Mom and Dad's Waltz . . . . **Lefty Frizzell**
He's willing to cry for them, and die for them, walk miles for them, and do chores for them, paying on a debt he believes he will always owe his parents.

Hungry Eyes . . . . **Merle Haggard**
A son watches his mother watching his father. Also on the Poverty list.

No Charge . . . . **Tammy Wynette**
A mother releases her daughter from debt—with just a little bit of Country guilt.

Mama, Don't Forget to Pray for Me . . . . **Diamond Rio**
A man fears his mother will be lulled by his apparent success into forgetting to pray for him. He knows (because of his fine home rearing) that he needs her prayers now more than ever.

Mama's Opry . . . . **Iris Dement**
A singer remembers her mother's song. She remembers watching her Mama hang clothes on the line, singing along to the radio as she sang to her daughter. She remembers hearing her tell of her grandfather fiddling and her grandmother allowing all of her furniture to be pushed aside to invite the neighbors over to dance. Mama's Opry is her daughter's Opry, too.

Love Without End, Amen . . . . **George Strait**
Earthly fathers are compared to God.

To Daddy . . . . **Emmylou Harris**
A self-sacrificing woman takes off as soon as the kids don't need her, leaving her husband just a note on the table.

Between Fathers and Sons .... Waylon Jennings

Fathers understand there are chances worth taking. Mothers try to protect. Fathers spend a lot of time scared.

When Mama Prayed .... Randy Travis

Things changed and big men caved. Mamas have a special relationship with God.

The Randall Knife .... Guy Clark

A son finds knowledge of his father while seeking knowledge of himself. Along the way, he damages a treasured possession. The damage and the silence surrounding it become an abiding gift of wordless, appreciative acceptance.

MY COUNTRY ROOTS

18 Soldiers

Soldiers are men—there's not a G.I. Jane in this bunch. Pro-war or anti-war, all these songs evidence both tremendous respect and sympathy for the soldier *and* for the friends and relations of the soldier.

Galveston . . . . Glen Campbell

Jimmy Webb's complexity-of-war masterpiece, is the most beautiful soldier-song in Country. A young warrior longs for home and love while acknowledging his fear of death. A love song to life, to a city, and—almost as an after thought—to a girl.

Heather, Are You with Me? . . . . Elizabeth Cook

Written by a woman and sung by a woman inhabiting the voice of a male bomber pilot thinking about his girl back home. This new millennium, "Galveston" asks the age-old intimate question, can war and love exist in the same heart? This song suggests that the answer might be no.

Fillipino Baby . . . . .Ernest Tubb

A boy from Carolina, far away from home, falls in love with a dark-faced girl while off to war. Tubb dropped the explicit references to race, but the darkness conveys.

Two Soldiers . . . . .Hazel Dickens & Alice Gerrard

Girls and women, sweethearts and mothers, are slaughtered in the silences that rise from battlefields.

Travelin' Soldier . . . . .Dixie Chicks

A young girl loses her innocence when a young man loses his life. The song evokes the origins of marching bands and the sweetness of piccolo players.

American Soldier . . . . .Toby Keith

Toby Keith sings of the man who encounters danger so that we will encounter peace, the American soldier, who is also a father, a lover, and a brother. It should be no surprise that old-fashioned country boys make excellent soldiers—farmers can't call in sick on Monday's either.

Arlington . . . . .Trace Adkins

Instead of going to heaven after death, a young soldier goes to the federal graveyard near Washington where his grandfather salutes him in greeting. A mature sense of the intertwining circles of male duty is jammed up hard against the image of a president who cries for every dead soldier—a fragment from a boy's abiding dream.

John Walker's Blues . . . . Steve Earle

An alienated American boy discovers Mohammed—a different "light out of the dim."

A Dear John Letter . . . . Jean Shepherd & Ferlin Husky

The day the battle ends, a soldier receives a letter from his sweetheart—written on the day of her marriage to his brother.

Riding with Private Malone . . . . David Ball

The ghost of a dead soldier is an unintended bonus, when a young man, safely returned from war, buys a used car. Is this a song about survivor guilt or balance in the universe?

War is Hell on the Home Front Too . . . . T.G. Sheppard

While her husband is away at war a woman takes the grocery boy as lover. It embodies the summer of '42 in three minutes and two seconds.

Dear Uncle Sam . . . . Loretta Lynn

A woman writes to Uncle Sam. He writes back a letter that begins, "I regret to inform you." Only one of the letters sounds sincere.

Something to Be Proud Of . . . . Montgomery Gentry

Much to his surprise, an adult son is told by his father that the every day heroics the son performs as a father and a husband are equal to the old man's World War II exploits.

GI Joe . . . . Waylon Jennings

An ode to an old World War II warrior. This GI Joe is as much defined by the music he listens to and plays as by the politics of his time. The old ideologies fit him about as well as his old uniform, but those ideologies and that uniform are what he went out into the world in and risked his life wearing.

Letters from Home . . . . John Michael Montgomery

A young soldier receives three letters: one from his mother, one from his sweetheart, and finally one from his father. The father's letter, in which he breaks his silence and announces that he loves his son, makes the soldier cry. It's formulaic, but the formula works.

MY COUNTRY ROOTS

19 Waitresses

Mama, working woman, exhausted creature, worthy temptress, beggar-lady, victim, whore or abundant lover—she's a walking, talking, standard Country character.

The Waitress Song . . . . Freakwater

This feminist, class lament contemplates the abstract—poverty as the anti-aphrodisiac, and the specific a uniform losing its color as it swirls in a coin-operated washing machine.

The Girl Who Waits on Tables . . . . Ronnie Milsap

This song depicts the waitress as an object. A girl waits at home for her cheating lover until she puts on a tight dress and starts waiting on, and perhaps for, a more appreciative audience. Her used-to-be man is left observing other men wanting what he once had. Possessed, lost, and still adored, the girl is a woman now—but the man doesn't get it. Throughout the song is a sense of the servile as erotic.

Instant Coffee Blues . . . . Guy Clark

A distant yet intimate encounter begins in a restaurant. This woman serves the coffee and picks up the check. But somehow this man seems to want something more than service—at least in the morning.

Trashy Women . . . . Confederate Railroad

This song explores the idea of a waitress as a wig-wearing temptress.

Is There Life Out There? . . . . Reba McEntire

It's the music video of this song that makes a waitress song. Frustrated by customers hitting on her, a waitress goes back to college. This waitress is a mother, a wife, and a person with ambition.

Eat at Joe's . . . . Suzy Bogguss

A bluesy, jazz track counterpoints the unromantic duties of the night, performed by women who are neither wives nor mothers, but are attentive in the short hours of the morning. Songwriter Matraca Berg, with her characteristic sharp-minded, big-hearted wit, captures the elemental sense of feminine abundance embodied by waitresses everywhere.

Beautiful Waitress . . . . Austin Lounge Lizards

Acid-drenched cynicism, snarled between bites of fine bluegrass picking and the repeated odd reference to crackers, asks us to consider exactly why it is that white-trash men enjoy the ladies who serve them chili. It has something to do with being seen, and something else to do with being missed.

Tip That Waitress . . . . Loudon Wainwright III

The audience can be heard laughing on this live record, something the waitress depicted in this song has very little reason to do. Wainright keeps us amused even as he reminds us that some Vietnam vets had children, and some of them grew up into women who get through graduate school despite shady chefs, pot-dealing bus boys, preening performers, needy mamas, and stingy patrons, as well as orders, glasses, forks, and spoons.

The Night's Too Long . . . . Patty Loveless

Sylvia moves from being a waitress to being a patron. Now she likes long nights.

Gatsby's Restaurant . . . . June Carter Cash

A country girl in the big city, with a horsetail and a yell in her mouth, pays for a rebellious adventure by washing dishes in Gatsby's restaurant. Washing dishes or riding in on a big white horse, any role's better than being a waitress.

The Girl Behind the Bar . . . . Flatt & Scruggs

The bar is a frame to display the pretty serving girl. When she steps out of the frame she is murdered. Being a waitress is a dangerous business.

MY COUNTRY ROOTS

20 Cowboys

Few symbols represent a complex American ideal as articulately and simply as this citizen of the plains. Beyond putting the "western" in Country and western music, these horse-riding heroes live in male communities beyond the laws of states, families, or God, Cowboys are often presented as being Texans, poets, singers, lovers, fighters, ramblers, and an endangered species.

El Paso . . . . **Marty Robbins**

The cowboy song to end all cowboy songs, this epic tale of heroic love and death portrays the chivalry that defines a cowboy's honor, and presents the Texas sound at its best. Robbins's writing and delivery brings the wild, dusty Old West to life.

Mamas Don't Let Your Babies Grow Up to Be Cowboys . . . . **Waylon Jennings**

Lending a bit of advice from his experience, Waylon warns mothers not to let their children become what he had become—and in doing so, he only further elevates the romantic idea of what it means to be a member of this nearly extinct breed.

Rhinestone Cowboy . . . . **Glen Campbell**

This cowboy has no interest in leaving the big city. He is an aspiring Broadway performer who dreams of fame and success while walking down the dirty streets of New York City. This song hit number one on both the Pop and Country charts.

Tumbling Tumbleweeds . . . . **Gene Autry**

This classic, performed by the original singing cowboy, compares the free life of a roaming cowboy to that of the aimless tumbleweeds blowing across the desert. Free, yes, but the moaning harmonies over the chorus melody reveal a deep loneliness.

Cattle Call . . . . **Eddy Arnold**

In this tribute to the cowboy, Arnold sings of a cool character roaming the range all alone, bearing the merciless elements, doing what he does best—herding his cattle with his sweet lonesome songs. Tough, for sure, but a little feminine, too.

I Want To Be a Cowboy's Sweetheart . . . . **Patsy Montana**

What lady doesn't love the cowboy or just want to be one? This yodeling cowgirl became Country music's first woman to sell one million records with this 1935 hit song, which won wide acclaim for its catchy celebration of the romantic frontier life.

The Red Headed Stranger .... Willie Nelson

The title song of a timeless song cycle, the mad main character shoots a woman for looking at the horse that his dead lover once rode. Testy, indeed. In Wild West fashion, he walks free and justified for his murderous actions.

Little Joe The Wrangler .... Bob Wills

Having run away from home, this stray orphan shows up at a camp out on the range and endears himself to the head boss, who teaches him everything he needs to know about being a cowboy—except how to avoid his fate, which would be riding his horse over a cliff.

Cowboy, Take Me Away .... Dixie Chicks

A contemporary take, this Dixie Chicks hit shares the same wish as Patsy Montana—a back-to-the-earth free and rambling life of love and romance.

When it's Lamplighting Time in the Valley .... Tex Ritter

A cowboy imagines his mother waiting up for him with a lamp lit in the window—a sign of welcome and hospitality. For some reason, it seems like this cowboy can't go home. This image of welcome becomes the image of loss.

Don't Take Your Guns to Town .... Johnny Cash

Sometimes a mother knows best, and here we see her taking Waylon's advice, begging her son not to be a cowboy and not to get himself in trouble. She knows that death is not far away and that it's out to get her son.

Faster Horses .... Tom T. Hall

In this tongue-in-cheek song, dialogue between a writer and an old cowboy leads to the realization that what makes the world go around is speed, sex, money, and a good twelve-year-old whiskey.

Which Way Does that Old Pony Run .... Lyle Lovett

An old cowboy's question. A young cowboy thinks he's guiding the horse like he guides life, but an old cowboy knows differently. Horses, like fate, go the way they are going; the only question is whether the cowboy can hold on for the ride.

MY COUNTRY ROOTS

Wild Horses . . . . **The Rolling Stones**

Any true cowboy relies on a heavy dose of chivalry to win-over the ladies when home from the range. This classic Jagger/Richards song reveals the only thing a cowboy loves more than his cowgirl are the horses he has yet to tame.

My Heroes Have Always Been Cowboys . . . . . **Waylon Jennings**

Jennings contrasts the hero-worship that children devote to cowboys to his adult lonely reality of roaming and living out on the range, or in his case out on the road. He is a survivor willing to admit his weakness. He has become his own hero, one he never quite expected. The cowboy the child aspired one day to be is not the cowboy the man has become.

Jimmie Rodgers and Hank Williams have more songs written and recorded about them than any of other artists. They have so many songs written and recorded about them that a small record label could release only Jimmy and Hank tribute records. This is ancestor worship, Country music style. Could this be another example of African influences in Country music? Country likes its tribute songs, but we'd like to see a few more about the women—Patsy, Dolly, Loretta, and Tammy.

The Train Carrying Jimmie Rodgers Home ...... The Nashville Bluegrass Band

The man who played the music before it had a name died on May 26, 1933 while recording in New York City. From Manhattan his body was shipped to Meridian, Mississippi. For many, watching that train pass by was as beautiful as the songs he sang.

The Night Hank Williams Came to Town .... Johnny Cash

If you lived in the South in the 1940s and '50s and Hank Williams came to your town, that was big time. Many men who attended his shows were inspired to pick up a guitar. Many of them also lost their dates to the members of his band, the Drifting Cowboys.

Are You Sure Hank Done It This Way? ...... Waylon Jennings

Songs about Hank often refer to the way things have changed in Nashville and in Country music. For many musicians the spirit of Hank Williams is an idealized one never to be recreated again.

The Ride. .... David Allan Coe

If you are a Country singer, your greatest dream ever would be for Hank Williams to pick you up on the highway in his Cadillac, drive you to Nashville, and let you pick his brain.

Midnight in Montgomery .... Alan Jackson

If ever a figure haunted Country music, it is Hank Williams. The ghost of the legendary singer, invoked ceaselessly in the music he helped to create, serves as a prophet of doom in this song.

If You Don't Like Hank Williams .... Hank Williams, Jr.

Of all the songs that Hank Jr. has written or sung about his father, this one captures the younger Williams's tendency to tell it like it is.

MY COUNTRY ROOTS

Cross Eyed Boy . . . . John Hartford

This one is an ode to the father of bluegrass music, Bill Monroe, who happened to be Hartford's mentor and dear friend.

Merle World. . . . . Jim Lauderdale

For those of us who have traveled to this state of mind, we know we never want to go back. But if we do, for some unforeseen reason, thank goodness for slow honky tonk ballads like this one.

Hey Willie . . . . Waylon Jennings

Always the outsiders, Waylon and Willie ultimately seemed isolated and alienated when the outlaw craze of the seventies became too popular and too commercial. This is a song from one dear friend to another, pleading for the days when life was simple and singing wasn't about fame.

What Would Waylon Do . . . . Joe Diffie

He hasn't been gone for very long and he is already man of myth within Country music; ironic because he fought celebrity and fame for most of his career.

No Show Jones . . . . Merle Haggard/George Jones

In the height of his battle with alcoholism George Jones gained a reputation for missing a few performances.

Alcohol and Pills . . . . Todd Snider

Sadly, many of America's great musicians have died in their prime as a result of addiction. Some would say it's the lifestyle, but others claim it's the price of fame. This somber song reflects on the latter.

Hank Junior Junior. . . . . David Allan Coe

Hank Williams Jr., for most of his earlier career, was considered to be just Hank's son, or Junior. That is until he became a legend in his own right, as is explained in this ode from a friend.

Grand Ole Opry . . . . The Nitty Gritty Dirt Band
(Featuring Jimmy Martin)

A song about the holy church of Country music. Controversial for some who play the music but are excluded from its hallowed walls, for everyone else who loves this music, the Opry is the cradle. Ironically, Jimmy Martin was never inducted into the society he so lovingly sings about here.

Old People

Country songs that tackle the subject of aging reflect both the counter-culture willingness to honor the village elder common in Country and the dominant culture fear and loathing of those closer to the end and death.

Old Five and Dimers Like Me . . . . Tom T. Hall

Sometimes we when we get on in years, we also get set in our ways. Most of the time, though, we've probably always been that way.

Yesterday's Wine . . . . George Jones & Merle Haggard

A seminal song about good friends, good times, and the benefit of a well-aged life.

Time Marches On . . . . Tracy Lawrence

It doesn't take long for time to slip away. One day your sister is in high school dating football players. In the blink of an eye she is a grandmother bouncing a baby on her knee. Hold onto what you got. Life changes fast.

Nineteen Something . . . . Mark Wills

A middle-aged man starts to realize that life is moving on as he ponders his childhood growing up in the 1970s and 1980s. He's not that old, but he's not that young either.

Back Side of Thirty . . . . John Conlee

Back in the day, being in your thirties was considered ancient by some Music Row standards. Now, for some, being in your thirties is just getting started.

Just like You . . . . Hot Rize

Between the subject matter and the bluegrass harmonies, this song will put you on your knees. When it comes to heartache, old folks are no different than anyone else.

Grandma . . . . Jon Nicholson

Looking at the back forty of life from the age of ninety-two, grandma realizes there is one thing she has yet to experience. So go ahead and twist her up one of those funny cigarettes.

Farewell Party . . . . Joe Nichols

Originally a hit for Gene Watson in the 1970s, the party mentioned is actually a funeral for a man whose last request is that the love of his life be there and pretend, one last time, that she loves him. It is a sad song, but beautifully rendered in this cover.

I'm an Old, Old Man (Tryin' to Live While I Can) . . Lefty Frizzell

Finally, he's got the money and he's got the time. Why then wouldn't all the women come running? Maybe it has to do with that cane and whitening hair, old man.

Hello in There . . . . John Prine

A touching song about a couple late in life and about the importance of taking a few minutes out of your day to stop and talk to an elderly person. Life gets lonely as we get older.

Rockin' Chair . . . . Jerry Garcia

This Hoagy Carmichael song is one of the most popular songs in the American songbook. A woeful, but gentle song, it examines the effects of age and the loss of loved ones. This version finds Jerry Garcia late in his life and appropriately resigned to the philosophy of the song.

Hurt . . . . Johnny Cash

Cash never turned his back on a good song. This song, written by Trent Reznor, front man for the alternative rock band Nine Inch Nails, shows Cash giving what could very well be his most emotional performance as he sings about the bitterness of life and the imperfection of man.

Wishing All These Old Things Were New . . . . . . Merle Haggard

He's an old man now. A man who experienced a lot of places and did a lot of things that are probably left unsaid, but it was a fun life and wouldn't leave anything out if he had it all over again to do.

Choices . . . . George Jones

Recorded late in this career, here George Jones takes on the dry subject of accountability. This cut will leave the hairs on your arms standing at attention. We are nothing but the choices we make, for better or worse. That my friends, is Country existentialism. This is a song for the ages.

What We Do

One way to understand Country is to say this: Country is working-class white American music. That doesn't say everything, but it says a lot. Country understands that it is defined by action and economics. Country is hard-pressed and responsible. As long as the woman and baby need you, you don't take the job and shove it. You work in shoes that do not fit to pay the rent and the baby sitter. Hard workers, country folk will play largely by the rules—even if some of them are unwritten. It's one of the ironies of the genre that Country (which can be unwaveringly pro-America) is probably the radio format that Karl Marx would listen to if he were alive and well, living in Tulsa.

23 Love & Money

Poverty in particular and money in general are everyday influences on Country love.

If You've Got The Money Honey, I've Got the Time . . . . Lefty Frizzell

Unabashed in his intention, this man is ready and willing if she's willing to shell it out—money that is. Other recordings of note: Willie Nelson.

Streets of Baltimore. . . . . Gram Parsons

Written by songwriting legend Harlan Howard, this song examines the potential risks of taking your small town wife to the big city with all its riches.

Long Black Limousine . . . . Glen Campbell

She left him seeking a life of limousines and big city nights. She finally gets her wish when she returns home in a hearse—a long black limousine. This is Country irony at its darkest and most sentimental. Other recordings of note: Merle Haggard and Elvis Presley

Big Harlan Taylor . . . . George Jones

Big Harlan Taylor has a brand new car, wads of cold hard cash, and the singer's woman. Early, classic George Jones.

Greenback Dollar . . . . J.E. Mainer

This song, with origins in the nineteenth century, exists in many different lyrical versions. All tell the tale of the woes surrounding a man who loses at love due to financial or social status.

MY COUNTRY ROOTS

Silver Threads and Golden Needles . . . . **Linda Ronstadt**

Recorded by numerous musicians, this gentle but firm song cautions that mansions and money can't mend a heart crushed by a cheatin' man.

Fourteen-Carat Mind . . . . **Gene Watson**

Women who have an itch for money and jewels can get the multiple men in their lives to do just about anything, from leaving their wives and kids to pawning everything they have.

Success . . . . **Loretta Lynn**

A woman is left in the ashes of heartache, all for the sake of her man's success. In her real life, success never destroyed Lynn's marriage of over forty years to her husband Doo.

Midnight Train to Georgia . . . . **Lynn Anderson**

This song was originally written by a Nashville-based songwriter about the break up between Farah Fawcett and Lee Majors as "Midnight Plane to Houston." City and mode of transport were changed in the lyric when it was first recorded, first by a little known soul act. This version is by a forgotten Country queen, Lynn Anderson. It was also recorded by Gladys Knight & the Pips.

Everybody's Sweetheart But Mine . . . . **Vince Gill**

Everything was fine until she went off and got famous and left her sweetheart behind. This song was perhaps inspired by his Gill's first wife, who was one half of the group Sweethearts of the Rodeo.

M-O-N-E-Y . . . . **Lyle Lovett**

One man's advice to another man regarding the art of attracting the woman with the ruby red lips. Texas big band with gospel background vocals.

That High Born Girl of Mine . . . . **Bashful Brother Oswald**

A guitar- and mandolin-driven song that proudly exclaims the love one man has for his higher-born half. A version by the same name sources from an African slave songbook.

24 | Cheating

A world that values marriage and family is particularly troubled by erotic passions that will not be constrained. Cheating songs are primary anxiety narratives in Country.

The Window Up Above . . . . George Jones

Is the protagonist of this song witnessing betrayal from the second floor window or from heaven? Regardless, she is cold, flat busted! George Jones wrote as well as sang this classic.

Slippin' Around . . . . Floyd Tillman

Tillman was called by some the original outlaw for his ability to push the stylistic boundaries of Country music in the 1940s. Some call this the original cheating song.

I May Hate Myself in the Morning . . . . Lee Ann Womack

Do it enough times and you start to know that it doesn't feel so good the next day. You're cheating despite knowing better, but you do it again and again.

You're Gonna Do Me Wrong . . . . Vern Gosdin

There is etiquette to cheating on your man. If you are going to do it, take the damn ring off your finger. Gosdin's voice, quivering and wounded in this slow song, is guaranteed to make you think twice about cheating and make you feel guilty if you do.

Wild and Blue . . . . John Anderson

Infidelity can be a vicious cycle of gratification followed by immediate disappointment. The male narrator of this song is patient, kind, and willing to take his fallen angel back in his arms, no matter her transgressions.

Daytime Friends . . . . Kenny Rogers

If your significant other doesn't seem to know someone all too well, maybe it is because they know him or her all too well.

You Ain't Woman Enough to Take My Man . . . . . . Loretta Lynn

Sometime the best defense against cheating is to be an amazingly good lover and to know you are. It doesn't hurt to let the other women know, too.

WHAT WE DO

Back Street Affair .... Webb Pierce

If he didn't tell you that he was married when the affair began, how can you believe him when he says it's all going to be all right from here on? A 1950s classic.

Feeling Single, Seeing Double .... Emmylou Harris

Throw a couple of drinks in her and she just can't help herself. She'll figure it out in the morning, though. The question remains *why* was she seeing double—too much to drink, or was it something else?

The Reasons I Cheat .... Randy Travis

Many men will admit they have jumped off of the fidelity train, but few will tell you why they cheated. This narrator tells why and in doing so, concedes that it very well might happen again.

When It's Springtime
in Alaska (It's 40 Below) .... Johnny Horton

A gold prospector comes in out of the snow and is wooed by the singer at the tavern. Everything is progressing nicely until the singer's husband shows up with a knife.

The One You Slip Around With .... Skeeter Davis

She's stuck in the rut of second chances. He's off cheating, but she's always there to welcome him back home. A simple ballad with silky harmonies.

We'll Sweep Out the Ashes in the Morning ..... Gram Parsons

We'll figure it out in the morning after we steal a little more love. A young Emmylou Harris sings backup on a perfect example of what Parsons called "cosmic American music."

Your Cheating Heart .... Hank Williams

One of the last tracks Williams recorded before he died, this song is an emblem for everything and anything adulterous in American popular culture.

25 Goodbye Love

Say goodbye to love—an honorable goodbye. These songs are monuments to abiding chivalry.

Bye, Bye Love . . . . .The Everly Brothers

This song was a huge hit in the 1960s for these sharply coiffed siblings. This version has a bubble gum, uplifting feel that works in sharp contrast to the lyrics of the song.

Ride Me Down Easy . . . . Waylon Jennings

If this does mean goodbye, remember me as a man of my word. A simple but poignant song about legacy and loss written by Billy Jo Shaver.

After the Fire Is Gone. . . . . Loretta Lynn & Conway Twitty

This song consistently finds itself on the various "greatest all-time Country songs" lists. More than saying goodbye, this song deals with the inability of two adulterous lovers to say goodbye to each other.

Hard Rock Bottom of Your Heart. . . . . .Randy Travis

For the cheating husband, the place between being welcomed home and being kicked out is the hell of un-forgiveness.

Goodbye. . . . . .Steve Earle

Sometimes when it is all said and done and the fighting has taken its toll, former lovers forget to even say goodbye. This truly heartfelt, tender song is accentuated by Earle's harmonies with Emmylou Harris.

For the Good Times . . . . Ray Price

This is a song that has been interpreted in nearly every genre of American music. Maybe it has to do with the fact that it is one of the few songs that tries to put a positive spin on parting ways.

The Last Thing on My Mind . . . Porter Wagoner & Dolly Parton

So often it is the case between two lovers that when things go bad, they decay until there is no chance for reconciliation. This countrypolitan duet has added drama and autobiographical implications in this recording between rumored old flames.

She's Gone Gone Gone . . . . Lefty Frizzell

She's never, never, never coming back, but that's what you get for cheating, cheating, cheating.

MY COUNTRY ROOTS

There Goes My Everything . . . . **Faron Young**

Recorded by numerous artists within Country, this version lulls and swaggers the way one might when all is lost and there remains nothing to hold on to.

The Distance Between You and Me . . . . **Dwight Yoakam**

This song typifies Yoakam's often sarcastic, dark wit when it comes to failed love. It comes dressed in Pete Anderson's unmistakable telecaster guitar riffs that punch you in the face.

Look What Thoughts Will Do . . . . **Lefty Frizzell**

Don't think about it, just do it. If you let your mind play tricks on you, you'll find yourself drinking with your shadow at the end of the dimly lit bar.

Oh My Sweet Carolina . . . . **Ryan Adams**

This song from *Heartbreaker*, his first solo album, Adams is joined harmonically by Emmylou Harris on this delicate goodbye to his home state, North Carolina.

Sad, Sad Music . . . . **Dwight Yoakam**

A man requests the full playlist of the broken heart. Unfortunately, the silence of goodbye is the only sound he hears.

Loving Her Was Easier
(Than Anything I'll Ever Do Again) . . . . **Kris Kristofferson**

You realize she is gone. You realize how complex your feelings are for this woman. Then what kills you is the realization that you will never have it that good again. You might want to avoid this song for a while if you just lost in love.

26 Dance With the Devil

There is a dark side to spirit and it will be encountered. Country, informed by the Bible, warns us against the devil in many guises.

Satan's Jewel Crown . . . . The Louvin Brothers

Off their gorgeous and tasteful record of spirituals *Satan Is Real*, the Louvins sing of a theme familiar to their Christianity—that only a lost soul can be found. Other recordings of note: Emmylou Harris.

Black Rose . . . . Waylon Jennings

In this classic Billy Joe Shaver song, the devil puts a married man under the spell of a shape-shifting mistress, the Black Rose. Now that there's no turning back, he is recounting his sins and begging for the Lord's hand to help pull him out of the darkness.

The Silver Tongued Devil and I . . . . Kris Kristofferson

Revealing and reveling in his double-identity, the man in this Kristofferson song battles the temptations of sex and sin waged by the sweet-talking devil beneath his skin.

The Devil Went Down to Georgia . . . . Charlie Daniels

Probably the best-known, and most-played song on the subject, Charlie Daniels turns the "crossroads narrative," a traditional story from the blues, about the mythological junction where a man is confronted by two paths, into a fiddle contest between a country boy and the devil. When the devil accepts defeat, Johnny gets his golden fiddle—and the legend lives on.

The Devil and Me BR549

A group that's always kept one foot on Country's original honky tonk roots, BR549 is joined by the Jordanaires on this feel-good gospel song about an intimate relationship between a sinning man and the devil. Admission is the first step to salvation.

The Devil and the Farmer's Wife . . . . Texas Gladden

A traditional ballad with roots in the British Isles, this light-hearted morality tale sung acapella exposes some negative stereotypes traditionally associated with powerful women—ultimately the farmer's wife is crowned stronger and better equipped to survive than the farmer.

WHAT WE DO

The Devil's Right Hand . . . . The Highwaymen

In this Steve Earle lyric, the Highwaymen sing about a boy who grows up worshiping the powerful allure of the gun, only to learn the hard way that mama was right—it's nothing but the devil's right hand.

Brokenheartsville . . . . Joe Nichols

With his sweet baritone, Nichols shows his old school roots, singing about a man who's had his love stolen by none other than the devil himself. Who knew Satan drives a Cadillac?

Ninety Miles an Hour Down a Dead End Street . . . . Hank Snow

What begins as an innocent kiss turns into almost certain death for this lover and his mistress. Here infidelity is compared to a reckless motorcycle ride with the devil.

It's a Sin to Tell a Lie . . . . Slim Whitman

The suggestion in this song is that the devil is never far away, and he has a way of fooling you—especially when it comes to love.

Angel Is the Devil . . . . Steve Earle

With a swing blues style that recalls early blues legend Blind Willie McTell, the man in this song has got it bad for a bad woman. Ultimately, it's the dark mystery beneath that binds him to her. Her name reminds us that Lucifer was once an angel.

Devil in Disguise . . . . J.J. Cale

Using his trademark swamp-boogie trance rhythms, Cale lures us into his life as a touring musician. Reacting to the long-standing stereotypes of music as the work of the devil, Cale embraces the myth, using his signature guitar style to cast us in his spell.

The Devil Had a Hold of Me . . . . Gillian Welch

Capturing the old-time sound and spirituality of Appalachian music, Welch warns against those who mock the power of the dark side, convincing us that this young girl has felt the devil's haunting touch.

Between the Devil and Me . . . . Alan Jackson

Sometimes all it takes is a real good woman to stand between a man and his tendency to make mistakes. Knowing that darkness is always near, Jackson seeks the shelter of his lover.

In this brutally honest admission of a constant battle with his demons, Cash describes a wild beast within the weak cages of his soul, and looks to his spirituality for rescue.

MY COUNTRY ROOTS

27 Honky Tonkin'

The church of hard drinking, hard times, and heartache. Music, whiskey, pheromones, and smoke are conducive to transcendence.

Honky-Tonkin' . . . . Hank Williams

The archetype for all related songs, Hank's invitation to "go honky tonkin'" is an irresistible repeated promise of smoke, sex, and alcohol. The rattle-trap acoustic rhythm section, whiney steel guitar, and his whiskey vocal paint a vivid picture of the wild joint he's headed to.

Wurlitzer Prize . . . . Waylon Jennings

The jukebox plays the same song all night long for the man who comes to the honky tonk—not to try and forget his lover, but to dance with her ghost and conjure her love.

Night Life . . . . Ray Price & Willie Nelson

A sophisticated anthem for the bar fly, this Ray Price tune associates the darkness of night with the broken dreams and old memories of those who seek a bar's shelter. Like Jennings, he both condemns his lifestyle and accepts it as who he is.

Turn it On, Turn it Up, Turn Me Loose . . . . Dwight Yoakam

In this boot-tapping tune, Dwight seeks the cure that a honky tonk offers—a place to drink, dance to good Country music, and sit and share hard-luck stories of life's blues.

Bright Lights and Country Music . . . . Bill Anderson

Hurt in a hangover of love, the man in this Whispering Bill classic knows of only one place that can make him feel better.

Swinging Doors . . . . Merle Haggard

Kicked out by his lover, the man in this Merle favorite tells his woman not to worry, that he has what he needs now at his new home. If she needs him, she'll know where to find him.

Honky Tonk Man . . . . Johnny Horton

Honky tonkin' gives this man everything he likes, including music, women, and fast times. What it doesn't give him is the stability he's left behind. Every night he has to go beg the woman he leaves at home for more money and a place to sleep.

Stoned at the Jukebox . . . . Hank Williams, Jr.

Sometimes the jukebox will provide the empathy no one else can. When darkness falls, he loses his mind and turns to the bottle and a song of his father's on the jukebox to help pick him up. But he just sinks down farther.

Bubba Shot the Jukebox . . . . Mark Chesnutt

There are times when someone plays a song on the jukebox and they probably wished they hadn't. In this song, the lyrics of a sad song mock this heartbroken man, so he goes to his truck, gets his gun, and unloads his aggression on the machine.

Hey, Hey Bartender. . . . . Del McCoury

Every bartender has heard a million stories about fools in love. The man goes seeking sympathy and realizes that no one knows loneliness like the bartender does. This version by McCoury shows what he learned under the tutelage Bill Monroe.

Honky Tonk Hardwood Floor . . . . Johnny Horton

This live recording from the Louisiana Hayride features Shreveport's favorite son, Johnny Horton, singing 'bout the honky tonk's allure.

Boot Scootin' Boogie . . . . Brooks & Dunn

Written by Dunn, this rockin' tribute to the line dancing typical of a Texas style honky tonk led to a number one hit and is representative of the duos raunchier roots.

Parallel Bars. . . . . Robbie Fulks

Riding that honky tonk steel guitar and telecaster, Fulks describes a tale of two lovers who unknowingly drink away their sorrows in bars across the street from each other.

Gin and Juice . . . . The Gourds

A Country-cover of Snoop Dogg's trademark single, the Gourds twang it up to create hip-hop honky tonk, revealing the party mentality South Central shares with South Texas.

Honky Tonk Heroes. . . . . Waylon Jennings

Waylon picked up where Hank left off in many ways. An ode to his younger years of hard timing and hard-drinking, he revisits memories of dancing and fighting his way through long nights at bars, lamenting the years lost along the way. The memory divides his conscience: one half dark, the other light, just like the arrangement.

MY COUNTRY ROOTS

28 | Courting

This term, archaic and anachronistic when applied to other radio formats is absolutely relevant in the world of Country.

Hey Good Lookin' . . . . Hank Williams

One of, if not the most classic and elemental, Country love songs of all time begins with simple flattery from a man who feels like he's got what it takes to cook up some homemade love.

Would These Arms Be in Your Way . . . . Keith Whitley

This song is sexy and honest in a candle-lit sort of way. Whitley's ability as a superb songwriter takes center stage as he politely poses a set of heartwarming questions.

Hit Parade of Love . . . . Jimmy Martin

Some argue that Martin is the greatest bluegrass singer of all time. Here, his vocals are both brazen, delicate, and pitched high in the sky, as he makes an attempt to top the charts in his true love's heart.

Gum Tree Canoe . . . . John Hartford

One would be hard pressed to find a sweeter courting song than this gentle and pastoral traditional tune about two lovers, a canoe, and the serenity of a slow moving river. Hartford's banjo playing conjures the flow and sound of a gently flowing stream.

Maybe Little Baby. . . . . George Jones

Propelled by a boogie-woogie piano and a fiery and quivering young George Jones, this song, like "Hey, Good Lookin'," slides towards the carnal edge of courting, where men court for the purposes of lust, not love.

Knock Three Times. . . . . Jack E. Ward

This crossover classic about neighborly attraction is more on the kinky and furtive side of courting, where voyeurism and secret signals in the night are the norm. The idea is driven home definitively in this version by the "wah-wah"of the electric guitar.

Slow Poke . . . . Pee Wee King

Stereotypes suggest that men tend to think of courting as a means to quick end—consent. They get impatient and anxious quickly when women force them to slow down.

You Move Too Fast . . . . .Elizabeth Cook

Stereotypes of women, on the other hand, suggest they like men who take things slow. This is a gentle track sung delicately and patiently . . . just like a woman.

Gold Watch and Chain . . . . The Carter Family

The second time around, courting often follows some sort of betrayal or malfeasance on the part of the one doing the courting or the one being courted. For this reason, success is a lot harder to come by, as is evident by the desperate attempts portrayed in this classic Carter Family song.

It Ain't Me Babe . . . . Johnny Cash & June Carter

The biggest risk in courting and falling in love is being spurned by the object of your desire. Never has rejection been so beautifully and delicately penned than in this Bob Dylan classic, sung, rather ironically, by the first couple of Country music.

Here in the Real World. . . . . Alan Jackson

The guy doesn't always get the girl and the girl doesn't always get the guy, despite what the movies may tell us. Realizing this is hard.

MY COUNTRY ROOTS

29 Rings

Rings—circles in the form of golden bands—have a little-noted prominence in Country. Most often appearing as wedding rings, they arguably function as symbols of commitment. In the Johnny Cash standard penned by June Carter Cash and Merle Kilgore, the golden band of love is a "ring of fire," in "Will the Circle Be Unbroken" the circle is eternity.

Golden Ring . . . . George Jones & Tammy Wynette

Displayed in a window, purchased in the pawn shop, slipped on a hand in a church, cast off in an apartment, and returned to pawn shop window again, a metal band is and is not a wedding ring. The presence or absence of love determines that. In this song, a ring is a metaphor for marriage.

Pawnshop Wedding Rings . . . . The Derailers

The Derailers understand what George and Tammy were singing about. This lover can't afford a new ring, but he thinks that their love can transform the second-hand pawnshop ring he offers into something of lasting value.

Does My Ring Hurt Your Finger . . . . Charley Pride

This man wonders if she's lost a bit of weight and her ring is too loose, or if there's something else making her leave the ring at home when she goes out at night. This is a song that reverses Country's traditional gender roles—here it's the husband who is waiting at home with worry.

Big Blue Diamonds . . . . Van Morrison

Love and a little band of gold or big blue diamonds and a cold heart? Morrison lends his Irish country soul to this story that pits *his* love against *her* money.

On the Other Hand . . . . Randy Travis

A ring can be a reminder not to cheat, even if you already have. This lover enjoys the immediate physical connection of his mistress, but his wife will always bring him home. Other recording of note: Keith Whitley.

Carrol County Accident . . . . Porter Wagoner

A son rushes to the scene of a car crash only to discover something in the glove box that forever changes his understanding of who his father was. He vows to keep the secret to himself, and preserves the local legend of his father's generosity and compassion.

Before the Ring on Your Finger Turns Green..... Dottie West

This man is as fake as the ring he is proffering. Take it from a gal that had his gold ring turn green on her hand, too.

Little Rock............................Reba McEntire

A more explicit retelling of a familiar theme. She's got all the money and the social position, but she doesn't get good lovin'. This lady's not slipping out to cheat, she's striding to divorce, and Reba paints her exodus as upbeat, easy, and sassy.

Ring on the Sill........................Cowboy Junkies

She takes off her ring; he slips it back on her. They balance being afraid of caring too much against the reality of losing that about which they care. A twinned image of a cocktail glass leaving a ring on the furniture puts ironic punk in the Cowboy Junkies' Country.

Ring of Fire...............................Johnny Cash

To enter love, to enter any circle of significance is a rite of passage bound by a symbolic ring of fire. Every ring is different. Merle Kilgore and June Carter Cash penned this elemental and complex hit immortalized by the man whose ring June wore.

Will the Circle Be Unbroken .... The Nitty Gritty Dirt Band
(Featuring All Stars)

Mother Maybelle Carter, Roy Acuff, Doc Watson, and other legendary Country icons join the Dirt Band in this song about the greatest ring, the circle of life completed by the circle of death. Like the rings in the other songs, the circle is transformed by love. One of the truly great songs of country music.

MY COUNTRY ROOTS

30 Divorce

To understand the power of Country lyric, you need look no further than this list. No other genre offers us as complex and articulate an understanding of this modern rite. Songs dealing with the dissolution of families and the suffering children; songs focused on divorce as an economic issue; songs centering on divorce as a response to erotic death, the creator of erotic possibilities, and the cause of erotic loss abound. This last notion might meaningfully be considered a peculiarly Country understanding.

D-I-V-O-R-C-E . . . . Tammy Wynette

Wynette spells out the truth. C-U-S-T-O-D-Y doesn't mean fun or play. Not then, not now. Tammy recorded this song in 1968. Unlike "Stand by Your Man," her bigger hit, this Bobby Braddock penned masterpiece remains relevant. Children still hate divorce and parents still try to hide it from them.

Mommy for a Day . . . . Kitty Wells

After the gossips in town brand her with a scarlet "A," a mother only gets to see her daughter on Sundays. Cheating women, or women even suspected of cheating, don't get much consideration.

Please Don't Talk to the Baby . . . . Razzy Bailey

There's a whole lot of Country songs about men wishing they were dead instead of in prison. This one is about a man wishing he was dead rather than divorced, after his ex-wife asks him politely not to talk to their son. Even wrapped up in precountrypolitan pseudo-slick sounds, this beast kicks like a stone-country mule.

(Pay Me) Alimony . . . . Rose Maddox and the Maddox Brothers

A hillbilly woman takes an economist's approach to divorce after advising women to stay single.

Going Through the Big "D" . . . . Mark Chesnutt

And he doesn't mean Dallas. This is the song for every man trying to make-out that he, not the woman, is the primary divorce-pain victim.

She Got the Goldmine, I Got the Shaft . . . . Jerry Reed

A gator-fried talkin' blues that finds a divorced man feeling a little used and abused by his divorce settlement. Hey buddy, you knew the rules going in.

All My Ex's Live in Texas . . . . George Strait
Ex-wives are scary people to be avoided.

Miss Being Mrs. . . . . Loretta Lynn
It's his body she misses. Back when good women didn't have sex
outside of marriage, divorce was a many-layered loss.

Sleeping Single in a Double Bed . . . . Barbara Mandrell
He's gone. And she's alone at two in the morning, stone sober,
wondering if she should have lied, or begged, to keep him. What was it
she wished she had said? Notice the use of the word "story," which in
Southern slang can mean "lie." How many women used this hook as a
pick-up line back in the 1970s?

Twenty Years and Two Husbands Ago . . . . Lee Ann Womack
It happens. What was unthinkable in a "good girl" song forty years
past, is now a mere time marker. This grown up woman is a "good girl"
and a "good mama" and twice divorced.

Release Me . . . . Ray Price
A passionate plea for a divorce from a marriage cold as a prison.

Release Me . . . . Dolly Parton
Marriage can be a cold prison for women, too. The same song as
Price's, but a completely different voice.

Homewrecker . . . . Gretchen Wilson
There's someone else behind this divorce.

Holding on to Nothin' . . . . Porter Wagoner & Dolly Parton
They're holding on with nothing left to hold on to. They are each taking
their share of the blame, and they both realize it's a body thing, not a
love thing. Pure Country, in three chords.

31 Jails and Prisons

There are songs about people sentenced to jail, enduring jail, or dying in jail; and songs that use prison as a metaphor to explore love and insanity as containment. Both kinds of songs have a central place in Country. Containment and confinement are anathemas to freedom-loving ramblers. Ironically, jail and prison are often the legal, if not natural, consequences of the wilder exercises of freedom. The jail and the prison are essential settings for Country, standing in stark opposition to the prairie, the garden, and the wilderness.

Folsom Prison Blues . . . . Johnny Cash

If he owned the railroad, the prisoner would be different. As he is, he shot a man just to watch him die. And now us coffee-drinking rich folk watch, through the prism of the song, the prisoner slowly die.

Stone Walls and Steel Bars . . . . Ralph Stanley & Friends

A man falls in love with another man's wife. One man ends up dead, the other behind stonewalls and steel bars, so tortured by love that he anticipates death as release.

Concrete and Barbed Wire . . . . Lucinda Williams

Williams evokes the image of love as a prison to suggest that physical walls of concrete and barbed wire are less significant than invisible walls of emotion.

I Got Stripes . . . . Johnny Cash

The man is marked by the judgment of law. Even his mother's presence does not alter the course of his increasing alienation. The onset of new deprivations further curses him, and the weeks come round and round in a downward spiral.

Way Downtown . . . . Doc Watson

"Just foolin' around" lands your butt in jail, with no one to go to for bail. It's a little like hell without redemption, and a little like the strangeness of life. At the center of the song, and the center of the strangeness, is Susie's sweet love and sweet song, as well as the knowledge that material wealth is neither forth coming nor significant.

I'm Just Here to Get My Baby Out of Jail . . . . Red Allen & Frank Wakefield

An old woman arrives at the penitentiary gates offering every service and every material possession in exchange for her son. He is released and she dies in his arms. Talk about going your bail.

Johnny 99 . . . . **Bruce Springsteen**

The usual elements of the Country jail song—a sweet mama pleading, a mean judge presiding, a preference for death over imprisonment—receive a new frame. This man, who confesses his thoughts are worse than his actions, makes a compelling case for mercy.

Still Doin' Time . . . . **George Jones**

Liquor as executioner, honky tonk as prison, infidelity as the crime, and the wronged woman as judge handing down the sentence.

In the Jailhouse Now . . . . **Jimmie Rodgers**

Similar to "Way Downtown" by Doc Watson, in this song the jailhouse is in fact literally "way downtown," and there's also a Susie in the narration. Here the foolin' around is of a darker cast (serious gambling), and the lovers end up in the jailhouse—together. This opens up the possibility that "In The Jailhouse Now" signifies "Just Got Married." Other recordings of note: Ernest Tubb.

Life in Prison . . . . **Merle Haggard**

Here, there is a double threat of prison—the physical jail and the jail of love-provoked insanity.

Women's Prison . . . . **Loretta Lynn**

A woman kills the other woman. Same old prison, same old wish for death, same sweet mama, except that mama's voice is the last sound the female convict hears before she is executed.

Nebraska . . . . **Bruce Springsteen**

A natural born killer finds a sweet girl willing to become a man-made killer. Ten dead people later, he's in a prison storeroom strapped to the electric chair wishing his baby were on his lap.

The Night the Lights Went Out in Georgia . . . . . **Reba McEntire**

Just when we were beginning to think that women don't kill, a sister kills her cheating sister-in-law only to have her brother end up in the electric chair. Vigilante justice backfires, creating a double murder. Why is the sister so concerned with her sister-in-law's infidelities, anyway?

Blackjack County Chains . . . . **Del McCoury**

A man condemned to a chain gang joins forces with his fellow prisoners and beats a sadistic guard to death with thirty-five pounds of chain—thus saving future prisoners from the guard's black snake whip.

Prisoner's Dream .... The Carter Family

A prisoner dreams of his wife with a rose in her hair and of his children being proud of their father. In his dream, shame lays shackled in the shadows.

Green, Green Grass of Home .... Elvis Presley

Curley Putnam's masterpiece. Putnam didn't just tell us about a dream, but he gave us the dream in all it's elaboration: a journey on a train to a sensual girl and welcoming parents; the hyper-pigmentation of the grass; the confusion of senses, the taste of color, the flashes of unadorned memory; the house, the swing; and finally the awakening to four gray walls the day before execution. We don't know what happened, we don't know why. We don't know if the prisoner is guilty or innocent. Are Mary and his parents still alive? We only know death is near and welcoming. This prisoner is free.

32 Coal Mining

Working in a mine is treacherous business. A miner endures confinement to help his family survive. To enter a mine is to be imprisoned, sent to hell and entombed. Or, is it an expression of manhood, of being able to support the family and of being woven into the fabric of your culture? There is nothing simple, pretty, or comedic about it. This is one of the few lists on which there are no songs that employ humor even as a subversive strategy.

Dark as a Dungeon . . . . Grandpa Jones

Jones captures the tragic conditions of mining though the metaphor of a prison in this archetypal song, warning future generations to stay away from the lure of the hellish mines.

Coal Miner's Daughter . . . . Loretta Lynn

In the song that stands at the center of her career, Lynn describes growing up in Butcher Holler, Kentucky with two hard-working, loving parents who raised eight kids on a miner's paycheck.

Miner's Refrain . . . . Gillian Welch

Welch captures the primitive essence of a miner's cold existence, and boils it down to his slaving everyday in a deep dark hole.

The Mountain . . . . Steve Earle

An earnest, hopeful story of pride and survival, the elderly coal miner in this song reports that the company has come and gone, taking the coal, the trees, and even his years—but they couldn't haul away the mountain, and that's his home.

Miner's Prayer . . . . Dwight Yoakam

In this beautiful ode to the memory of his grandfather, a long-time Kentucky coal miner, Yoakam presents the fear and despair that followed the men and families who earned their living underground.

Blue Diamond Mines . . . . Jody Stecher & Kate Brislin

This song highlights the lack of stability or job security that mining provided its aging workers. Dependent on the income, older miners would be betrayed by both the companies and the unions, left with no options but to take big pay cuts to retain their jobs.

WHAT WE DO

Coal, Black Gold . . . . .The Country Gentlemen

The sentiment expressed here is a common refrain in all of these songs—many a man was lured into the mine by the promise of good pay and an end to poverty, and many a man died with little to show for it.

Black Lung .The Strange Creek Singers

Hazel Dickens raises her voice, one created by the West Virginia coal mining culture, in protest of the disease that claimed the life of many a miner.

Prayer of a Miner's Child . . . . .Dock Boggs

Having witnessed the toll of mining on a father, the child prays here for God's mercy and intervention. The song is presented as you might have heard it up in the Blue Ridge Mountains, mid-century.

Coalminers . . . . Uncle Tupelo

A contemporary take on an age-old problem, this song takes an activist approach, trying to rally the miners out of the darkness they're accused of giving into. Problem is, they need to support their families and aren't easily coaxed out.

Miner's Blues . . . . The Carter Family

This lyric chooses to focus less on a specific narrative than it does the psychological despair that accompanies a life in the mines.

You'll Never Leave Harlan Alive . . . . Patty Loveless

The place most Americans associate with the tragedies of coal mining, Harlan County, Kentucky, claimed many a miner's life. In this Darrell Scott lyric, the child of a miner traces her roots home only to realize that she's the only one in her family to make it out alive.

I Wouldn't Live in Harlan County . . . . .Wayne Scott

A son has left his home far behind, sacrificing and struggling to save his own life, but the ghosts of Harlan still haunt him.

Quecreek . . . . Buddy & Julie Miller

National coverage of the 2002 Quecreek mining disaster in southwestern Pennsylvania revealed that America's dark relationship with mining wasn't a thing of the past. This is a stirring retelling of the story that ended in the rescue of nine miners who were trapped underground for over three days.

Paradise . . . . John Prine

In the sense that some make the case that slavery gave rise to jazz and the blues, one can make the case that coal mines gave birth to much of the character of Appalachian culture. Despite the deprivations, the death, and the natural devastation, Prine makes the audacious claim that the place he once called home was and still remains paradise.

MY COUNTRY ROOTS

33 | Abuse

Country songs provide a kind of intimate fictional documentation of the suffering that goes on in some homes. From the twinned acknowledgements that the sadism present in some homes rivals and eclipses the sadism in many jails, and the courage present in many homes rivals and eclipses the courage present on many battlefields, rise some of the most shining feminist moments in the genre. Many of these songs are intended not to inspire their listeners, but to direct them, literally and specifically. Every hurt woman and child has a home in Country. An escape manual is as close as your car radio. By directly attacking the invisibility of family beatings, killings, and rapes, and by giving narrative shape to these events, Country removes some of the high walls they hide behind.

Rosie Strikes Back . . . . .Roseanne Cash
Eliza Gilkyson wrote these upbeat, life-saving directions for leaving: don't pack, grab the baby, get gone.

Concrete Angel . . . . Martina McBride
A little girl's bruises are hidden by linen and lace.

The Little Girl . . . . .John Michael Montgomery
Mama does drugs; Daddy drinks. Daddy shoots Mama and then himself while little girl hides behind the couch. Surprise ending makes you wonder if there's a Jesus.

Born a Woman . . . . .Sandy Posey
According to this song, to be born a woman is to be born controlled and hurt—"a woman's place in this old world is under some man's thumb." She's so controlled and hurt, she thinks she likes it.

A Man's Home Is His Castle . . . . .Faith Hill
This woman's home is a cage. When the police can't help her, she decides to buy a gun. All the strings in the world can't take the strong out of this sticky sweet song.

A Broken Wing . . . . Martina McBride
A woman who has taken too much abuse, "Lord, he loved to make her cry," flies out a window. Suicide as freedom? Some say she leaves him, some say she jumps.

Independence Day . . . . Martina McBride

With her man inside and her daughter safe outside, a woman burns down her own house.

Are We There Yet, Mama? . . . . Walter Hyatt

A woman escapes an abusive "mean old man" with her kids in a "piece of junk." You can almost hear "Rosie Strikes Back" on her car radio.

Ask Me . . . . Amy Grant

A man rapes his daughter, uses her as "his little rag." But the woman makes it to adult in one piece, remarkable for her grit and optimism.

Letter to Mom . . . . Iris Dement

A young woman writes a hard letter revealing that once upon a time, a long time ago, when she was ten years old, her mother's boyfriend molested her.

Goodbye Earl . . . . Dixie Chicks

Mary Ann and Wanda kill Earl (with faux kindness and poisoned black eye peas) after he violates a restraining order—beating Wanda so badly that she ends up in intensive care. The girls keep happy and busy with their own little roadside jam business while the police keep looking for their missing man. Country girls can survive.

WHAT WE DO

34 Hard Questions

Veiled behind many actions and words lurks the query, "Do you love me?" The problem is, the right answer, "I love you," is too easy to fake. There is a sub-genre of Country love songs that addresses this problem. Posing "love riddles," hard questions designed to provoke revealing answers, this list would make a good pre-nup Q & A for any one contemplating marriage

If I Needed You . . . . Don Williams & Emmylou Harris

Written by the great Townes Van Zandt and immortalized by Williams and Harris in this stirring duet, this song poses a simple question. Some of the hardest questions to answer are the most simple.

Would You Lay With Me in a Field of Stone. . . David Allan Coe

There isn't a more serious and difficult set of questions than the ones posed in this David Allan Coe song. It is rumored that he wrote this for his brother's wedding day. It'd be tough not to get nervous hearing this one at the altar.

If I Were a Carpenter . . . . The Seldom Scene

Do you love me for who I am or for what I do? This is a great song for the person who thinks their lover is out to dig gold. Made popular by Joan Baez in the sixties, many people today know the version sung by Johnny and June Carter Cash, however, it's tough to beat the harmonies in this bluegrass version by the Seldom Scene.

Will You Miss Me When I'm Gone . . . . The Carter Family

You knew the Carter Family would weigh in on this category. The first family of Country sings about a speaker who wonders, "will our love last when I die?" The call and response simultaneously poses the question and the demand.

Are You Teasing Me . . . . Carl Smith

In this classic, reminiscent of early Hank, Carl Smith—a.k.a. "Mr. Country"—questions his lover's sincerity as if he doesn't deserve it.

Why Don't You Love Me
Like You Used To Do . . . . Hank Williams

From questioning love to being flat-out baffled by love, this upbeat, swinging standard features Hank's playful lyric wizardry on top of that rattle-and-trap, early honky tonk sound.

If You Were The Woman And I Was The Man . . . . **John Prine**

In this gender-bender, Prine harmonizes with The Cowboy Junkies' Margo Timmons, wondering if things would be any different in this relationship if the roles were reversed. Now that's deep, and kinky, to boot.

Why Can't He Be You . . . . **Patsy Cline / Loretta Lynn**

In another case of confused identity, Patsy and Loretta both recorded versions of this Hank Cochran classic. Everything in this woman's relationship is just fine, except the good man isn't *her* man.

Will You Be Loving Another Man . . . . **Bill Monroe**

The father of bluegrass music is looking for a straight answer to a very practical question: *"Will you be true or not?"* It's a question every male musician asks before he heads back out on the road.

If I Were The Man You Wanted . . . . **Lyle Lovett**

In this melancholy lament of love unaligned, Lyle answers an unasked question in order to provide himself the comfort of knowing that love presents the most paradoxical answers.

Are You Tired Of Me, Darling . . . . **The Carter Family**

The hard questions continue, even for those who have a long marriage or relationship and this is one of the hardest of all: Has love lost its step over time? The doubt communicated in Mother Maybelle's vocal balances the sweetness of the lyric.

Why Baby Why . . . . **George Jones**

Jones is at his best here, questioning his lover/jailer about his emotional imprisonment. One of Country's great and simple lyrics encounters a greatest performance. Other recordings of note: Webb Pierce.

WHAT WE DO

35 Sweet Invitations

As long as there have been songs, there have been singers wooing a lover with romantic propositions. Here, we gathered some of Country's sweetest invitations.

Walk Through This World With Me . . . . The Seldom Scene/ Tammy Wynette

The proposal of a lifetime, this ode to love and devotion makes the perfect wedding tribute. Versions by both the Seldom Scene and Tammy Wynette are amazing. Perhaps, one for the woman, and one for the man?

Come On In (And Make Yourself At Home). . . . . Patsy Cline

A platonic love song about missing the old hometown, where folks don't lock their doors and everyone greets you with a smile. What could be a sweeter invitation than the neighbor saying, "Come on in and sit right down and make yourself at home"?

Hello Stranger . . . . Hazel Dickens & Alice Gerrard

Sung so sweetly here by mentor and student, it'd be hard to notice that in all likelihood, this is a song about a hard luck prostitute looking for a little love from one of the rounders in town. A timeless Appalachian rendition of an A. P. Carter classic.

Lets Chase Each Other Around the Room . . . . . Merle Haggard

Evoking that great Tulsa Swing sound, Merle's hit adds a playful, child-like angle to an adult wish, offering the remedy for any "grown-up" relationship gone cold. You have to admit, the song is pretty convincing.

Let's Make Love . . . . Faith Hill

Invitations don't get simpler or sweeter than this. A lesser voice or sparser production would leave this invitation a bit too explicit. Here, it's so silky and sweet it leaves the listener wondering, "Is that nice girl really saying this?"

Please Come to Boston . . . . David Allan Coe

This man is out on the road, dreaming of a better life in another town. When he begs his wife to join him, promising all the dreams each city offers, she stands her ground and gives him a sweeter invitation: Come on home to the woman who loves you most.

Wallflower, Wallflower . . . . **Bob Dylan**

The setting could be a junior-high dance or a dirty old bar. "I'm standing over here looking at you all the way over there, and both of us don't want to be here, so why don't I take you home?" Does he ever get the guts to speak to her?

Making Memories of Us . . . . **Keith Urban**

The basic invitation here is, "have a future with me." This song is a long series of sweet invitations interspersed with sweet promises.

Lay Lady Lay . . . . **Bob Dylan**

Dylan *did* have a way with wooing the girls. Off of a big-selling crossover record that featured Earl Scruggs, Johnny Cash, and Norman Blake, this song may be the best known and the sexiest "sweet invitation" in all of Country music.

Help Me Make It Through the Night . . . . **Kris Kristofferson**

Kristofferson wooed many a young woman with this timeless song, taking a feminine approach to a masculine problem: I need you, but just for the night.

MY COUNTRY ROOTS

36 Alcohol

Liquor is clearly the drug of choice in Country. Companion, change agent, or catalyst, addiction or liberating ritual, the significance of drinking alcohol is one of Country's most abiding concerns.

There Stands the Glass . . . . Webb Pierce

For some who dwell within the misery of a broken heart, there is no more valuable tool than the vessel, which holds and administers the fluid that eases the pain. This ode to the glass was a number one hit for Pierce in 1953. Other recordings of note: Van Morrison.

I Gotta Get Drunk . . . . Willie Nelson

One of Nelson's original demo recordings from the early 1960s, this upbeat and seemingly playful ode to the inevitability of insobriety is, if nothing else, blunt. Think of it as a true representation of the inner monologue of drunks just before they pull up a stool at the bar.

I Drink . . . . Mary Gauthier

One of the most poignant Country songs about alcohol and identity from one of its current songwriting masters, this story assesses the realization that we are who we are—warts and all. Gauthier's intimate delivery convinces us that the darkness can be sweet.

Since I Started Drinking Again . . . . Dwight Yoakam

Depending on the person, becoming a drunk can take some time. Doing it for the second or third time, though, takes no time at all. Ironically, this is one of those songs that will have you tapping your feet even though it is about despair and futility.

Tonight the Bottle Let Me Down . . . . Emmylou Harris

One of the inherent risks of drowning your sorrows on a bar stool is that sometimes those memories you're running away from pull up a seat right next to you and match you drink for drink.

If Drinking Don't Kill Me . . . . George Jones

No other Country performer can get the whisky in his voice through your ears and into your blood like George Jones. Not only is this one of THE drinking songs in the pantheon of Country, but it also has the greatest drunkenly image: passing out on the steering wheel of your car early in the morning only to wake up the neighbors with the car horn.

Backsliders Wine . . . . **Michael Martin Murphy**

This is a perfect example of the Country as paradox. In this song is a deep philosophical concept conveyed through simple lyrics. Often, we drink in hopes of changing the situation, but in reality we can only change or not change ourselves.

Don't Come Home Drinking
With Lovin' on Your Mind . . . . **Loretta Lynn**

You stumble home after seven beers and an evening with your buddies and you're ready for a roll in the hay. She's not having any of it. Next thing you know, you're sleeping on the couch. Don't mess with Loretta.

Misery and Gin . . . . **Merle Haggard**

This could serve as the quintessential barroom lament. Moral: Some of the most crowded bars are the emptiest places, and gin, although good with tonic, is best mixed with misery.

Whiskey Lullaby . . . . **Brad Paisley (with Alison Krauss)**

A tragic story of bad love and slow suicide, delivered in this stirring Krauss duet. Using alcohol as a medicating cure for one's emotional ills is always dangerous, and sometimes fatal.

Skid Row Joe . . . . **Porter Wagoner**

This is the theme song of the drunk and downtrodden alter ego that Porter Wagoner created for himself in 1970. The album cover is a portrait of Joe slumming behind the Ryman Auditorium, the theater that made Wagoner a celebrity.

Straight Tequila Night . . . . **John Anderson**

The first thing tequila affects is the mouth, specifically the words that come out of mouth. Anderson offers some good advice for anyone looking to court the broken-hearted woman who favors tequila. Buy her a glass of Chardonnay.

Tear My Still House Down . . . . **Gillian Welch**

Moonshine has always been one of the great exports of the Appalachian Mountains. For some it was a steady source of income, but for others, like the narrator of this lament, it was a curse of damnation and ruin.

MY COUNTRY ROOTS

Yes, I Guess They Oughta Name a Drink After You . . . . John Prine

Every man with a penchant for drink who has lost at love has felt this at one time or another. The genius of this song is that it is loosely performed and written, almost as if there had been a few cocktails served before the audio engineer hit the record button.

Cocktails . . . . Robbie Fulks

It is thought by some that the origin of the word "cocktail" comes from the fact that they were originally a morning drink, one you might enjoy to the crow of the rooster. A countrypolitan staple written by Bill Anderson, performed here by the leader of the current postmodern Country scene in Chicago.

Alcohol. . . . . Brad Paisley

Booze is personified and given the opportunity to weigh in on its own global legacy. After all, it has influenced our world leaders and provided white people the ability to dance.

37 Drugs (Illicit)

Better known, and perhaps better accomplished by rock and hip-hop artists, explorations of cocaine, heroine, morphine, and marijuana nevertheless have a significant place in Country. Where are all the methamphetamine songs?

Willin' ....Little Feat

A delicate inducement becomes a glorified anthem to the synergy of hard working and hard partying. The combination of long lonely days and nights driving a big rig across the country leads this trucker to a dependence on various drugs and alcohol—whatever it takes to just keep moving—preferably "weeds, whites, and wine."

Cocaine Blues............................Johnny Cash

Cash is at his best when he is both devil and angel. This brutal narrative starts with a speedball and a murder, and ends with a convincing plea to let alcohol and narcotics alone.

Let the Cocaine Be................ Doc and Merle Watson

Picking up where Cash left off, Doc carries the message of this song with his smoking guitar playing and soulful harp blowing. A fun, foot-tapping take on addiction that suggests if one can quit cocaine, there's always corn liquor to drink.

Sam Stone .... John Prine

Prine's moving take on the psychological toll that the Vietnam War exacted on its survivors, He wrote the chorus from a child's perspective, capturing both the naivety and the horror of watching a father die from a morphine overdose.

Holdin' ....Jamie Hartford

In this song, the son tastefully recreates a moment from his father's groundbreaking 1971 release, "Steam Powered Aeroplane." This playful song delves into the cryptic lingo and camaraderie requisite among marijuana smokers.

Illegal Smile .... John Prine

Another ode to weed and a favorite sing-along of his devoted fans. This Prine song captures the element of disguise that being stoned provides its users.

Just Dropped In to See What Condition
My Condition Was In . . . . **Kenny Rogers**

Who said Kenny Rogers was a square? Here he rocks. While the drug of choice isn't specified, the delusional disorientation of the main character and the psychedelic production style suggests we're dealing with more than just alcohol.

My Morphine. . . . . **Gillian Welch**

Dressing the drug in the metaphor of a lover, Welch describes addiction as a love affair gone wrong, and brings the hazy-high to life with a woozy-yodel that features gorgeous harmonies with David Rawlings.

Take a Whiff On Me . . . . **Woody Guthrie**

A variation of the previous song. In this song, cocaine addiction is taken to a psychological extreme in which the speaker's euphoria creates a semi-sexual desire for affection. Also interesting is the reference to the longstanding practice of injecting race horses with cocaine to increase their performance.

Sinaloa Cowboys. . . . . **Bruce Springsteen**

When two brothers steal away across the Mexican border, they find the steady work they'd been hoping for in a California orchard. They also find something they didn't expect: the methamphetamine that eases their pain, and eventually kills one of the brothers.

Quaaludes Again. . . . . **Shel Silverstein**

A one-of-a-kind, hilarious tribute to this heavy-hitting pill made popular in the 1970s. The prolific poet and songwriter, Shel Silverstein, steps up to the mic and delivers an undeniable vocal performance, culminating in a fall-on-the-floor-laughing dialogue between a frustrated husband and his very stoned wife.

Needle and the Damage Done . . . . **Neil Young**

Young has always toed the line between Country and Rock 'n' Roll. This timeless tribute to the tragedies of heroin abuse is without rival.

38 Trains

Sometimes trains are a drug metaphor. Sometimes trains are a sexual image. Sometimes a train is a death metaphor. Sometimes a train is a train. The innovation that opened the west and doomed the wilderness is the same innovation that took us away from home and brought us back. In Country the train is a central image, symbol, metaphor, and reality.

When the Train Comes Along . . . . Uncle Dave Macon

Filled with good cheer and optimism, this song paints the train depot as a setting of great hope. Trains often brought good news and good people to otherwise secluded places. Macon, born in 1870, was one of the first stars of the Grand Ole Opry.

Ruben's Train . . . . Doc Watson

This fast-paced, banjo-driven song from the old-time mountain songbook about a man and his train has a mournful and tragic feel. Other recordings of note: Dock Boggs.

Wabash Cannonball . . . . Boxcar Willie

One of the most popular train songs in American music, this song dates back to the nineteenth century. This imaginary train was an important part of hobo mythology.

Freight Train . . . . Elizabeth Cotten

Freight trains carry the heavy loads. The singer is inspired that they still travel fast and she's counting on that truth to make her escape from the weight of the pain she carries.

Fireball Mail . . . . Roy Acuff

Trains were the war-horses of industry and society pre-World War II. With their power and promise of progress, they became machines of myth in early Country music. Written by Acuff's legendary publishing partner, Fred Rose, here it is sung by arguably the most famous train song singer.

I Heard that Lonesome Whistle Blow . . . . Hank Williams

This might be the most mournful Williams song. It tells the story of a man locked in a cell, doomed to listen to the lonesome whistle of the train that took him away from his sweet heart forever—the train that will never bring him back.

WHAT WE DO

Rock Island Line . . . . .Johnny Cash

For over a hundred years, this train ran from Chicago out as far as Colorado and New Mexico. This tribute to the train became a standard in the Country and Folk genres. Cash's version is spirited and just plain fun.

Orange Blossom Special . . . . .The Stanley Brothers

This passenger train ran from New England to Florida, and was the first to travel to the sunshine state. Here, the fiddle is played to mimic the train rolling down the track.

City of New Orleans . . . . Willie Nelson

This song, which memorializes the train from Chicago to New Orleans was written by legendary Chicago songwriter, Steve Goodman. Nelson won best song Grammy in 1984 for his version.

Can't Stop a Train . . . . The Derailers

Like a speeding train, you can't stop a heart once it starts breaking. This song echoes the Bakersfield sound made famous by Buck Owens.

Big Train from Memphis . . . . .The Seldom Scene

For many who grew up in the first half of the century, seeing a train for the first time was a defining moment. This bluegrass song features rich harmonies and the unmistakable sound of Mike Auldridge's dobro.

My Baby Thinks He's a Train . . . . .Roseanne Cash

Here the train metaphor rides on the back of a man who pulls into woman after woman like trains pull into town after town. Any tramp in town can take a ride.

Long Black Train . . . . .Josh Turner

The only train we all must ride is the one that takes us from this life to eternity. Turner's warm vocals make it sound less frightening, though.

39 Murder

When it comes to innovative ways and places to kill people, no other genre holds a candle to Country. Rooted in the tradition of murder ballads, a form of story song brought to America from the British Isles, these tales cover a myriad of murders of passion, pride, protest, and pain.

Caleb Meyer .... Gillian Welch

In a haunting voice (reminiscent of the Carter Family) Gillian Welch sings of a woman who defends herself from brutal rape by slashing the drunkard's throat with a broken bottle. Sounds like a black and white Smokey Mountain horror film.

Little Sadie .... Doc Watson

In this traditional tale, which also goes by the name of "Bad Lee Brown" and "East St. Louis Blues," a man shoots down his lover, Sadie, then flees the crime scene with requisite regret. His punishment: an alliterative sentence of 41 days, 41 nights, and 41 years.

The Snakes Crawl at Night .... Charley Pride

Murder Ballad 101: Man catches wife cheating. Man murders wife and lover. Man sentenced to die. Strangely, an upbeat, almost spiritual rendition here by the venerable Pride.

Knoxville Girl. .... The Country Gentlemen

One of the oldest Appalachian murder ballads is particularly disturbing for its grisly details and pathological narrative of a man who murders a girl because he loved her "so well." John Duffey's high tenor vocal recalls the Louvin's immortal rendition.

The Ballad of Charles Whitman .... Kinky Friedman

Written and performed by the self-proclaimed "Jewboy from Texas," this satirical song sheds light on one of America's first mass killing sprees. What a story it is.

Highway 29 .... Bruce Springsteen

A dark tale of murder and suicide from a master of American gothic, and the New Jersey cowboy, Bruce Springsteen. The man falls for the woman, a bank robbery goes terribly wrong, and on the run, they drive off a cliff. Was it an accident?

The First Mrs. Jones .... Porter Wagoner

This song addresses a recurring commitment in many of the old murder ballads: If I can't have her, then nobody will. This husband warns the second Mrs. Jones not to run out on him, or else.

Fair Margaret and Sweet William............. Tim O'Brien

One of the original Child Ballads brought over from England and popularized in Appalachian culture. This haunting tale is about a double suicide. In its original form it explains the origins of the rose.

Rose Connelly .... Texas Gladden

In this field recording of Rose Connelly, captured by Alan Lomax, she sings of a woman poisoned by a man who thought he'd inherit all her money. Boy, was he wrong. This song is also commonly referred to as "Down In The Willow Garden" or "The Willow Garden."

Pretty Polly .... The Stanley Brothers

No one sings about death like Ralph Stanley. In this gruesome narrative, the young man woes his lover away on horseback for a romantic ride through the mountains. When they come to a valley, there lies a freshly dug grave—hers.

Tall Lover Man......................... June Carter Cash

Leave it to June Carter Cash to rewrite the murder ballad from a woman's perspective. When this woman's lover says he'll never leave his wife for her, she stabs him and her guilt leads her to stab herself, too. There's a lot of Johnny in June's voice here.

Cabin Among the Trees .... Jeff White

Flat-picker and bluegrass singer Jeff White shares this story about a rambler seeking shelter from a driving mountain rainstorm. When he knocks on the door of a lonely cabin in the pines and is refused shelter, the blood spills.

The Thunder Rolls........................ Garth Brooks

A woman waits all night worried about her husband apparently caught out in a storm. When he arrives, the scent of perfume in the air turns relief to murderous rage.

Delia's Gone .... Johnny Cash

The Man in Black focuses not so much on the act and the details leading up to murder as the psychological torture and deep regret a man lives with after having killed the only woman he loved.

L. A. County . . . . **Lyle Lovett**

Lovett takes the traditional form and updates it into a dark story of love gone wrong. Jealousy and misery drive this man to shoot two young lovers at their wedding altar. Whereas many murder ballads resolve with the killer's regret, this murderer has none.

Banks of the Ohio . . . . **Doc Watson**

Rejection can be tough to take. After turning down a proposal of marriage, a woman is stabbed and thrown in the river.

WHAT WE DO

40 Executions

Execution songs are ironically American.

25 Minutes To Go . . . . .Johnny Cash

Quirky gallows humor animates this death row "partridge in a pear tree" —except instead of counting back to Christmas, we're counting down to death. Cash refuses to give us any redemptive ending, just the death scream's final syllable, as the prisoner dangles at the end of a rope.

Sing Me Back Home . . . . Merle Haggard

On his long march to death, a condemned prisoner requests that a fellow inmate sing him a song that will revive old memories and conjure the comfort of home one last time.

Long Black Veil. . . . . Lefty Frizzell

A tragic story of mistaken identity and infidelity, this is Country's best execution ballad. A man, wrongly-accused of murder, refuses to reveal his alibi. The secret he took to his grave: he'd been cheating with his best buddy's wife. The gallows pole is easier to swallow than admitting he had betrayed both his friend and his wife. Narrated from the other side of the grave by the dead man. Other recordings of note: Johnny Cash.

Dead Man Walkin'. .Bruce Springsteen

Here, death is "a pale horse." The guilty man doesn't beg for forgiveness, instead he chooses to wrap himself in the darkness and totality of his sin. Absolute in its lack of mercy, cruel in its objectivity, this song was inspired by the movie of the same name.

Send My Body . . . . .Randy Travis

Another man is convicted of a crime he didn't commit, but this one seems to take his impending execution quite well. The judge seems to think he should be ashamed, but his innocence and his faith keep his mood lifted. All he wants is a proper funeral train and a good burial under "Mama's apple tree." Family and fame transcend all else.

The Gallows Pole . . . . Tex Ritter

Mama to the rescue again. In this country blues standard, the hangman must be bribed with silver and gold. While his sweetheart, his father, and his best buddy all fail him, it's his mother who arrives with everything she has to free her doomed son. Other recordings of note: Led Zepplin.

Miss Otis Regrets . . . . **Katy Moffatt**

A favorite song of female vocalists from Ella Fitzgerald to Linda Rondstadt, and written by the great Cole Porter, this story puts the woman at the mercy of the executioner. When Miss Otis is abandoned by her lover, she shoots him down, and a mob hangs her from a weeping willow tree. The understated irony of the chorus only magnifies the tragedy.

Johnny 99 . . . . **Bruce Springsteen**

A young man sentenced to ninety-nine years in prison begs for the judge to show mercy by executing him instead. The prisoner's argument is a convincing one: His thoughts are much worse than his actions, and he deserves to be put out of his misery.

Bad News . . . . **Alejandro Escovedo**

This itinerant outlaw seems to stir up trouble wherever he goes, and has a particular knack for eluding the law. When the authorities finally catch up with him in Oakland, he pulls his most impressive escape— slipping the noose-knot mid-hanging and living to tell the story.

Tom Dooley . . . . **Doc Watson**

A traditional song based on a true story—the 1866 murder of Laura Foster in North Carolina. Dooley refutes his guilt over and over even though the facts prove otherwise. The refrain reminds him that there's no escaping the fate he's been handed.

Promises . . . . **Lyle Lovett**

When you've lost all control, words lose their meaning and power. A solitary meditation on the hard reality of facing execution, Lovett nearly brings the impossible-to-imagine to life. This is a realistic psychological portrait that explores a true human response to an immovable date with state-sanctioned murder.

Turn It On, Turn It On, Turn It On . . . . **Tom T. Hall**

When the doctor diagnoses this man as mentally unfit for duty, the local town folk ridicule and mock him for being a coward. In an attempt to prove them wrong, he sets out on a massive killing spree, until he's brought in and sentenced to the electric chair. His last words are the title of this epic story-song and his hope for salvation.

WHAT WE DO

41 Love Begs

This list conveys the honesty and sentimentality that have become the bread and butter, the brilliance and the bane, of Country songwriting. Getting the balance right has a lot to do with precise control of tone and the significance of the truth told. If praying is a lot like begging, begging is a lot like praying, and there are a lot of lovers who enjoy being worshiped. That significant, if troublesome, truth is what brings this list to life. Love begs.

Make The World Go Away . . . . Ray Price

Hearing the desperation in Price's whimpering vocal, it'd be hard not to forgive this man, no matter what he'd done. The reality of regret is too much take. A track characteristic of the Nashville sound associated with the Bradley/Atkins production styles of the 1960s.

Today I Started Loving You Again . . . . Merle Haggard

Merle's sweet baritone reminds us that sometimes the first step to recovering your lover is admitting that you've been wrong. Now he's just gotta figure out how to get her back.

Come Back . . . . The Derailers

No contemporary Country band knows how to honky tonk better than this Austin, Texas band. In this sassy call-and-response shuffle, the boogie-woogie telecaster is evidence of rock 'n' roll's influence on the genre.

Love Please Come Home . . . . Old and In the Way

In this straight up bluegrass standard by the crossover super group featuring Rowan, Grisman, and Garcia, there'll have to be forgiveness before anyone's coming home.

Love Has No Pride . . . . Bonnie Raitt

And apparently it has no shame, either, which is what makes the lyric here so brutally painful. When love chooses us, it can be a difficult thing to shake. Raitt has always had a way of keeping two feet in the Blues and a hand in Country.

Who Were You Thinking Of . . . . Texas Tornados

A tongue-in-cheek take on questioning just where a lover's imagination travels during sex. This tex-mex all-star group fronted by Freddie Fender and Doug Sahm not only won over listeners in Mexico and the U.S. alike, but also won a Grammy. A great two-step!

On and On . . . . .Bill Monroe

There's not so much begging here as stalking; when you know what you want you gotta go get it. There's something about the persistence of the character that suits Monroe.

Two-Dozen Roses . . . . Shenandoah

Trying to win back the love he took for granted, this man misses the mark. You get the feeling that it isn't the flowers or wine she's interested in, but a good man.

Please Come Back With My Heart . . . . .Levi Mullen

This Arkansas cowboy has laid guitar tracks on the records of Merle, Willie, Dolly, and George. He also happens to be one hell of a honky tonk performer. Here he's soaked in beer and begging for his lady to return what's rightfully his.

Please Come Back, Darling. . . . . .Del McCoury

When you think bluegrass tenor, Del McCoury is second only to the father of the style, Bill Monroe. Adding a darker, mountain-tinged tone to his entreaty, McCoury sings of a man broken with despair over losing his wife. He begs for her to come back to life.

If I Can't Have All Of You
(Give Me What . . .). . . . . The Wilburn Brothers

Suffering from the delusion of love and rejection can lead to some pretty irrational behavior. Here our spurned lover begs for whatever she's willing to give him, and whatever that is, he will be satisfied.

Don't Close Your Eyes . . . . Keith Whitley

It's sad and embarrassing when a lover realizes that his or her lover imagines old flames while making love. Sometimes just asking him or her to stop will work and that could be a good thing for all involved.

How We Feel

In Country, emotion often trumps reason. To thrive and survive in the territory of Country, an evolved heart just might serve you better than an over-programmed mind. Country embraces the notion that there is no, or little, objectivity. Everything is filtered through a lens of emotion, a lens that provides a Country song with passionate and detailed observations. There is little neutral territory in Country feeling; there's a lot of intensity and a lot of articulation, and there are heaps of joy and pain. Some interpret the joy as insincere, and others find the pain immature. However, Country sounds authentic to many familiar with struggle and survival.

42 Crazy

Nobody does crazy better. Maybe it's because the South has a special place in its heart for eccentrics, or maybe it's because Southerners and country folk understand sanity as a kind of prison while worshiping those that cross over the line dividing insanity from sanity as freedom fighters. Maybe Country is rich in crazy because poverty and low social status conspire to break minds.

Crazy . . . . Patsy Cline

Where better to start a list of insanity than with this torch song from a mad lover, written by Willie Nelson and immortalized by Patsy Cline? A heavy spell of romantic passion and regret sweeps through this twisting chord arrangement and immortal lyric.

I Don't Remember Loving You . . . . John Conlee

A man looses his mind, quite literally, after he loses his woman, who is now visiting him in the loony bin. Conlee's gruff, soulful voice lends sincerity to such an oddly chilling story of amnesia.

He Stopped Loving Her Today . . . . George Jones

Arguably, the best Country song of all time—a heaping mountain of love and crazy, penned by Bobby Braddock. Nothing changes, except that death comes. This man is a true promise keeper. We call this dynamic stasis.

Break My Mind . . . . Linda Ronstadt

This woman warns her lover that if he gets on that plane and leaves her, she'll go insane. This version showcases the 1970s Country Rock popularized by Gram Parsons and The Flying Burrito Brothers. Don't miss Roy Orbison's version either.

Crazy Arms . . . . **Ray Price**

Insanity manifests itself in the alienated body of this broken-hearted lover. You can hear the madness in his wavering voice. Price scored big with this 1956 hit, which captures his shuffling, East-Texas, honky tonk sound. A Country music classic.

Hello Walls . . . . **Willie Nelson**

So far gone, the man in this song has lost his love and his mind as he makes fast friends with the inanimate surroundings of an empty room. Never before did windows, walls, and a ceiling have so much feeling.

Mama He's Crazy . . . . **The Judds**

A daughter explains to her mother that he might be crazy, but he's crazy for *me*. With Wynona's beautiful voice, you don't have to be crazy to love her.

She's Crazy for Leaving . . . . **Rodney Crowell**

One man's crazy is his woman's sanity. He tried to stop her from leaving, but she blew out of town so fast she left his truck wrapped around a telephone poll. The Texas boogie sound in this tune captures the high-speed and high jinx that ensue.

Doctor Good Doctor . . . . **Guy Clark**

A humorous spoken-word song in which a session with a shrink is compared to a date with a lady who rents by the hour. The session is the second best hundred dollars he ever spent.

Committed to Parkview . . . . **The Highwaymen**

Cash penned this song about the addictions, demons, and human spirits that circle around an upscale in-patient Nashville mental-health facility. Hearing all The Highwaymen together on this track should convince any dabbling user to quit.

I'd Have to Be Crazy . . . . **Willie Nelson**

Willie's holding hard to his sanity in this lyrical ode to cowboy madness and true love. Arguably one of Nelson's most beautiful and peculiar songs, it also features one of his most personal and engaging vocal performances.

I Fall to Pieces . . . . **Patsy Cline**

An integrated whole shatters into many broken parts in this dedication to the mental devastation that lost-love can wreak on its victims.

MY COUNTRY ROOTS

Dream-like and a fine example of the early "Nashville sound," this song sounds best crooning from an old jukebox.

Miss Emily's Picture . . . . John Conlee

A gentleman suffers from a broken heart as well as obsessive/compulsive disorder. Very scary.

The Rubber Room . . . . Porter Wagoner

Absolutely peculiar, this spooky and slightly-hallucinogenic song from Wagoner transports us to the dark interiors of a haunting asylum, where lost souls struggle for their mental lives. Inside the padded cell is a place to be feared and a place to confront fear.

Suspicious Minds . . . . Elvis Presley

When jealousy takes root, paranoia takes over—one of many ways that loving someone too much can cause you to spiral into madness. Draped in multi-layered late-sixties production, Elvis cannot hide his Country roots in this immortal performance.

43 Country Erotica

Working in a tradition as old as the song of songs, Country is a wild, willing, and unabashed engagement with the carnal beneath the winking eye of God. An underlying sense that sex is nice, not naughty, is a primary connection between country folk and the hippies.

The Golden Rocket . . . . Hank Snow

Trains have always been a metaphor for sex. This train chugs furiously down the line from town to town, breaking hearts everywhere it goes.

Black Snake Moan . . . . Leadbelly

Sung by one of the great Country Blues artists of all time, this song about the liability between a man's legs has been covered by many in Country, most notably Jimmie Dale Gilmore.

Between You and the Birds
and the Bees and Cupid . . . . Pee Wee King

This song was recorded in a time when it was appropriate to use code for acts performed behind closed doors. Translated into today's language, it says she rocked his world in the sheets.

Let's Do Something . . . . Vince Gill

A young boy promises all the spoils of life and love to a young girl if she will just climb out that window and "do something" with him. The driving, honky tonk feel of the song tells you what that "something" might be.

Son of a Preacher Man . . . . Dusty Springfield

This seminal crossover classic tells the steamy story of a young girl and her lordly lover in a case of religious passion seen in a new light.

Private Conversation . . . . Lyle Lovett

As long as only you and I know about this, that shade gets pulled down, and you get over in this bed with me, we should be just fine. After all, as far as they know, we were just talking. Right?

Tonight I'll Be Staying Here With You . . . . Bob Dylan

From one of the only albums Dylan recorded in Nashville, this sweet and gentle love song proclaims the power of a woman's touch.

MY COUNTRY ROOTS

Rollin' in My Sweet Baby's Arms . . . . Doc Watson

Made a classic by the bluegrass duo Flatt and Scruggs, this sing-a-long seems innocent enough on the first listen. I guess everything having to do with making love seems innocent in the beginning.

Love to Lay You Down. . . . . Conway Twitty

The king of erotic, lovemaking songs describes his favorite thing to do. It's a god-blessed thing to *want* to lay your woman down in her housedress and curlers.

Key Lime Pie . . . . Kenny Chesney

Who eats key lime pie while shooting rum and strumming a guitar on a barstool in the Caribbean? Believe me, no forks or knives were needed when dessert was served.

Come a Little Closer Baby . . . . Dierks Bentley

Come here, baby. I know how to heal your pain and I think you know how to heal mine. Song's video matches the lyric step for step in steam.

There's More Where That Came From . . . . . . Lee Ann Womack

A willing woman and a willing man in a motel room that no one knows about. The first time is always better the second time around, that is, until the guilt and anguish sets in.

When You Say Nothing at All. . . . . Keith Whitley

Passion is often best demonstrated using every part of the body, with the exception the vocal chords. Other recordings of note: Alison Krauss.

44 Existential Despair

Despair. Alienation. These songs are a report from rock bottom, but rather than inspiring you to get out the razor blades, they inspire the getting over yourself and getting on with life.

I'm So Lonesome I Could Cry . . . . Hank Williams

A Country masterpiece, this song's simple, stark expression of depression's darkest depths is quite literally in a world of its own. Arguably the most important song in Country, it is also one of its most recorded.

In the Pines . . . . Leadbelly

Performed here by its originator, Huddie Ledbetter, this song reveals the inexorable bond between Country and blues, and describes a depression without end. This spurned lover has lost all hope and reason.

A Thousand Miles from Nowhere . . . . Dwight Yoakam

What Leadbelly understood about alienation, Yoakam seems to get and respond to in this song that reveals that a world without time is a world without reason and purpose. There's a more driving and upbeat styling here, but the sentiment is still despair.

Man of Constant Sorrow . . . . .The Stanley Brothers

Repopularized by The Coen Brother's film, *O Brother Where Art Thou*, we return this song to its origins—a recording by Virginia's Stanley Brothers. Written by the elder Carter, but sung by younger brother, Ralph, the heard irony of harmony co-existing with alienation is arresting.

Sitting Alone in the Moonlight . . . . Bobby Hicks, Doyle Lawson, J.D. Crowe, etc.

In this lament of lost love, the expression of alienation lies in the character's mad obsession with the night sky up above, which mocks his sorrow. This is a good example of Monroe's often-overlooked lyrical and poetic prowess.

Speed of the Sound of Loneliness . . . . Nanci Griffith

The distance between loneliness and dreadful sorrow is not very far at all, especially when you're talking about spurned love. John Prine wrote this wonderful song.

MY COUNTRY ROOTS

Stop the World and Let Me Off . . . . **Dwight Yoakam**

There's no beating around the bush with this song: not only is our spurned man done playing love's games, so too does he seem to have lost his will to live. Depressing, yes, but you can dance to it.

'Til I Gain Control Again . . . . **Rodney Crowell**

Less about giving up hope, than it is about asking for help in the midst of giving up hope, this song proffers an antidote to existential despair: honesty coupled with surrender. Other recordings of note: Emmylou Harris.

Slow Rollin' Low . . . . **Waylon Jennings**

Waylon brings his Country-funk style to this Billy Joe Shaver song about facing life without anyone around to comfort and care for you. Shaver's unique poetic prowess is honored and showcased on this, *the* outlaw record, *Honky-tonk Heroes*.

If Loneliness Can Kill Me. . . . .**Loretta Lynn**

Safe but not snug in her homey, honky tonk surroundings, Loretta Lynn describes just how lethal loneliness can be.

I'll Never Get Out of This World Alive . . . . **Hank Williams**

While Hank would sing a spiritual now and then, he often chose alienation over salvation. With his masterful sense of humor and witty lyricism, he ponders the ultimate truth: there's no escaping death.

Which Way Do I Go . . . . **Waylon Jennings**

A unique expression of alienation, this guy's sitting on the side of the highway watching all the cars and the lights fly by in the night, looking for the way he seems to have lost.

I'm No Stranger to the Rain. . . . . **Keith Whitley**

Spurned and cursed by life, this fellow is used to things going wrong. If you go head-to-head with the devil and win, you are truly some kind of bad.

45 Empathy

Everybody likes to listen to a story or a song that they can identify with—so too do the characters here. For the postmodern readers out there—behold, our *meta* list. This is the list of Country songs about Country songs.

Mr. Jukebox. . . . . .Ernest Tubb

The drunk man in this bar just heard a song that told his life story, so he raises a glass and makes a request to the man inside the machine, spinning all those records.

Mr. Record Man . . . . Willie Nelson

When this man heads to the local record store to look for something he'd heard on the radio, his description is pretty vague. All he can tell the store owner is that the song made him feel like he wasn't the only one down in love.

Hillbilly Fever . . . . .Little Jimmy Dickens

A mainstay of the Grand Ole Opry, Little Jimmie Dickens hit it big with this tune that reveals "hillbilly" isn't just for country folks. If you're not careful, even those in New York City will be swept away with the Country-wide epidemic.

Hey Mister, That's Me Up on the Jukebox. . . . . . James Taylor

From empathy we shift to reality—imagine you don't *feel* like the guy singing on the jukebox, but that it's really *you*, and if you hear it one more time, you might just die. Other recordings of note: Linda Ronstadt.

Jones on the Jukebox . . . . .Johnny Bush

In this tribute to the power of a good song, Johnny Bush sings about the man who needs his George Jones all the time. How many of Jones's title's can you find in the lyric?

Vinyl Records . . . . .Todd Snider

In this song that could've been titled "Record Rap," Todd Snider shares what he's got in his record collection. It sure beats a static press interview about influences.

Them Old Love Songs. . . . . Waylon Jennings

Why can't life be like it is in the movies or in those happy Country songs? A sweet, drown-in-your-sorrows song from Jennings, as he dreams that he can love and be loved in return—like the couples in those old love songs.

Acuff-Rose . . . . Uncle Tupelo

In this song from alternative-Country favorites Uncle Tupelo, records baring the original Acuff-Rose catalog label provide a man the love and partnership that no lover could.

Lorena . . . . John Hartford

A song that was the favorite request of Confederate soldiers during the Civil War may also be the oldest song in our collection. Here it is performed by one of America's great music ethnographers and songwriters, John Hartford.

Play a Train Song . . . . Todd Snider

In a playful, gothic tale of friendship, Snider reminds us that there's nothing like a train song, especially when life feels like it's blurring down a one-way track. Anyone who has ever played the Radio Café in Nashville has heard Skip Litz call out between songs, "Play a train song!" Maybe someone up in heaven will play him Todd's.

If Hell Had a Jukebox . . . . Travis Tritt

This record would be in it. This man suffers sorrow when his woman walks out and leaves him wishing for a jukebox full of sad songs to keep him company in the hell his sorrow has led him to.

Don't Rock the Jukebox . . . . Alan Jackson

When you're heart-broke and looking for something to make you feel better, nothing helps like a sad old Country song—not that he doesn't like rock 'n' roll, he's just not in the mood right now.

I Hate These Songs . . . . Dale Watson

This clever song lists several classically-sad Country songs in an attempt to point out that many peoples' favorite songs are the ones that make them feel the worst.

46 Desire

These are the odes to the lovers, to the wishes and dreams that are just out of reach, and the hellish feelings of dissatisfaction they wreak on us all. In Country, amorous and erotic desire arise within the frame of larger economic, historical, and cultural poverties.

Walking After Midnight . . . . Patsy Cline

This woman may or may not be doing more than walking after midnight, but her search is all about finding the man she had, not who or whatever else she encounters out on the lonesome road under the dark of the moon.

Dear Someone . . . . Gillian Welch

In this gorgeous, lullaby/prayer, the lonely dreamer builds a boat and floats it out to sea, in search of the lover they have yet to find. All we can do is hope they find what they're looking for, though we fear desire has led them astray.

Sailin' Around . . . . John Prine

Sailing on the high seas, the ever-frustrated character in this song has finally found the lover he's been looking for, but can't reach her. He keeps sailing after her. A male modern version of "Walkin' After Midnight."

Girl on the Billboard . . . . Del Reeves

This fun tongue-twisting song is our Country version of John Keats's "Ode On A Grecian Urn." A big-rig driver yearns for the larger-than-life, beautifully painted girl on the billboard he passes everyday. No matter how hard he tries, she'll never come to life. Yet, every time he passes her, he breaks from the inadequacy of his life into the beauty of imagination. Desire, imagination, and creation are close cousins.

Greensboro Woman . . . . Townes Van Zandt

A man prefers the imagined embrace of a woman a thousand miles away to the real embrace of the woman before him here and now. The shelter of desire leads to responsibility.

Unwanted Sign Upon Your Heart . . . . Hank Snow

The worst part of desire is thinking you actually might have a chance to get what it is your heart wants. The man in this upbeat Hank Snow song learns that the hard way.

HOW WE FEEL

I Can't Help the Way I Don't Feel . . . . Waylon Jennings

Desire is a two-way street, but the love is only going in one direction. This woman desires the man who wishes he could say the words he cannot. They're both left wishing it weren't so. There's a lot of tough love all around here.

Stone Wall . . . . Red Allen

In this bluegrass standard, Red Allen relates just how hard it can be to try to reach a woman's heart when she's built a wall up around it. Not only is his love unrequited, but his questions of "why" also go unanswered.

Sonja . . . . Lyle Lovett

Lovett steeps in his desire for this young woman pouring his coffee at the bar. However, she's got her eyes on his friend, and he can't write the song to sing to get her attention. Unrequited desire deals him a double-blow.

Weary Blues from Waiting . . . . . Darrell Scott and Tim O'Brien

Desire has exhausted the man in this song. He has been sitting at his window, for what must be seasons, looking for a sign of his lover's return. You get the feeling that he'll be waiting forever, and a person could die of waiting.

Mississippi Woman . . . . Waylon Jennings

A strange, cinematic song in which desire leads to voyeurism. A jealous man paddles around the swamp to watch the woman he loves meet another man for a secret rendezvous.

You Are My Sunshine . . . . The Carter Family

The Country song about "desire," co-written by the governor of Louisiana, Jimmie Davis, this song laments the loss of the woman who was everything happy and bright in his life. He dreams she's in his arms, and hopes that she'll return; if not, this desire may turn from depression into suicide. Who can live without sunshine? This is desire for the most basic needs in life.

47 Love Hurts

"Ouch!" in the land of extreme metaphors. This psychological reality gets sincere and simple, matter-of-fact treatment in Country.

Drivin' Nails in My Coffin .Ernest Tubb

She's not hurting him so much as she's *killing* him in this signature Tubb tune—hell, she's *already* killed him; the drinking just seals his fate.

Stop the World and Let Me Off . . . . Waylon Jennings

This lover's been left high and dry by his woman, and now that the pain of heartache and alienation has set in, he wants off—off the planet, that is. This song proves that when you have got the right words, you don't need a lot of them.

Pins and Needles in My Heart . . . . . . The Nitty Gritty Dirt Band
(Featuring Roy Acuff)

This Fred Rose song uses the suggestion of a voodoo doll to bring this man's heartache to piercing life. It's performed here with a particular sadness by Roy Acuff during the *Will the Circle Be Unbroken* sessions with the Nitty Gritty Dirt Band.

Walking the Floor Over You . . . . Merle Haggard

This man's been left to pace the lonely halls of his mind, suffering the psychological pains of heartbreak and love lost.

I Love You So Much It Hurts Me . . . . Floyd Tillman

When you love so deeply, you realize that you can lose so deeply, too—just thinking about it hurts. An early cross-over innovator, Tillman croons away on this Texas-styled waltz.

Crying. . . . . k.d. Lang

Sung in her distinctive torch-lit alto voice, Lang examines the only real tool that one has when love truly hurts.

Heartaches by the Number . . . . Ray Price

The "inverse proportion of love rule" states: when one of two lovers' feelings for the other grow at equal rates, but in opposite directions, somebody's gonna get hurt.

I Don't Feel Like Loving You Today . . . . Gretchen Wilson

Sometimes love hurts so bad you want to take a day off. Tough.

I Ain't Been Right Since You Went Wrong . . . . .Ernest Tubb

Grown men just aren't supposed to sit at home and cry like this fella, who can't do anything right since his woman up and left him.

South of Cincinnati . . . . Dwight Yoakam

In this gorgeous ballad, she has been writing the same letter to him everyday for fourteen years. He, on the other hand, is in Chicago, drunk in a lonely apartment. Together they are doomed to never really say what they feel.

Love Hurts . . . . .Gram Parsons

The classic Parsons duet with Emmylou Harris swings from one extreme to another as youthful idealism shatters into a thousand pieces of harsh, almost cynical reality. Getting your heart crushed is a sure way to grow up fast.

48 Hot

These Country songs are not-so-innocent. It's all about the senses, here and now.

You Show Me Yours and I'll Show You Mine .... Willie Nelson

A drunken proposition from someone that, if they were lucky enough to find a willing partner, wouldn't last two minutes before passing out. From the movie *Honeysuckle Rose*.

Get Your Biscuits in the Oven . . . . Kinky Friedman

A tongue-in-cheek critique of women's rights from an openly chauvinistic man who only wants to be fed and felt by his bra-burning wife.

She Thinks My Tractor's Sexy . . . . .Kenny Chesney

A bucket full of chicken, sweet tea, and a ride on a John Deere tractor. It doesn't get much kinkier than a farmer fetish, but we would have left out the bit about a "teeny-weeny ride."

Passionate Kisses . . . . Mary Chapin Carpenter

Good, strong lovemaking isn't a need. It is a demand. This song, written by Lucinda Williams, proves that even Ivy League graduates can be sultry.

Behind Closed Doors . . . . Charlie Rich

This 1970s countrypolitan classic by the "Silver Fox" is a favorite of women who *seem* so lady-like in the living room and so appropriate at parties.

Morning Ride. . . . . .Lee Greenwood

Nothing gets a day going like a little love. This sultry, steamy number from a singer best known for his patriotic ballads will make you wish the sun was coming up all of the time.

Slow Hands . . . . Conway Twitty

This song examines a different kind of healing hands—slow, tender, patient, yet deliberate.

Baby's Got Her Blue Jeans On . . . . .Mel McDaniel

Isn't it amazing what a simple, tight pair of jeans can do to the male libido? No other pair of pants can break a man down by just walking down the street.

MY COUNTRY ROOTS

Somebody's Gotta Do It . . . . .Elizabeth Cook

A woman has needs too, and as long as you give what you take, everyone wins in the end. Right?

Let Old Mother Nature Have Her Way. . . . . .Carl Smith

The first husband of June Carter Cash has got one thing on his mind in this song. Men are apt to promise anything in the world just to get a little.

Dynamite . . . . .Brenda Lee

There's something extremely risqué, bordering on improper, when you realize that Lee was just thirteen years old when she recorded this song in 1957.

Don't Make Me Come Over
There And Love You . . . . George Strait

I dare you to dare a man or a woman who hasn't been intimate in a while with a suggestive look. This is a Texas two-step with a little Latin flare.

Hotter Than the Mojave in My Heart . . . . .Iris Dement

After hearing this song from DeMent's debut album *Infamous Angel*, it's hard to look at an apple pickin' cart in the same way.

Don't You Make Me High . . . . Van Morrison

The leg bone connects to the thighbone, which connects to the . . .

49 Revenge

Sometimes forgiveness isn't the course to take. When they've been done wrong, Country folk will cast a spell, conjure a curse, and seek revenge.

Cry, Cry, Cry . . . . Johnny Cash

Cash reminds his lover that actions have their consequences. Ready to give up on his good-timing woman, he at least has the good heart to warn her that a sea of tears is coming her way when she finds she's all alone.

Blue Moon of Kentucky . . . . Elvis Presley

Elvis covers the oft-misunderstood Bill Monroe classic—full-blooded call for revenge on the woman who's left him all alone. Now that she's gone he conspires with the elements to avenge his loss.

These Boots are Made for Walking . . . . Loretta Lynn

This version is a little more sinister than Nancy Sinatra's. Here, the warning is clear—keep it up and she's gonna stomp on your head on her way out the door. You go, girl.

The Curse. . . . . Dwight Yoakam

A chain-rattling arrangement and a series of curses are cast at a woman who cursed a man with love.

If You Don't Love Me Somebody Will . . . . Carl Smith

Good stuff here from Carl Smith in this groovy-sounding honky tonk tune. He's loud and clear: If you don't want me, I'll sick jealousy on you.

You're Gonna Change or I'm Gonna Leave . . . . . Hank Williams

An ultimatum more than a curse, he loves her enough to leave instead of revenging himself on her in culturally accepted, but nonetheless abusive, ways.

Keep Your Distance . . . . Buddy & Julie Miller

Buddy and Julie Miller are at their best in this hard-driving song, warning the irresistible tempter to stay away or else, when really they're praying that they will just stay far away.

Shame on You . . . . Spade Cooley

Sometimes the worst revenge is the self-inflicted kind. The man in this song puts a little salt in the wound.

HOW WE FEEL

MY COUNTRY ROOTS

Lesson in Leavin' . . . . Jo Dee Messina

The childish character of revenge is revealed in this sassy song with schoolyard imagery.

Here's a Quarter, Call Someone Who Cares . . . . Travis Tritt

Sometimes the best revenge is a cool quip and twenty-five pennies.

Seven Curses . . . . Bob Dylan

A slight departure from the list, this tragic epic of a father's love for his daughter ends in a series of seven severe curses levied on the wicked judge as he hangs the father.

50 Before and after the "Big D"

Life seems to come apart at the seams before and after the "Big D." The significance of marriage to the listeners of Country is underscored by a body of songs that explore and capture the period just before and just after divorce.

Sister's Coming Home . . . . Emmylou Harris

Her man's done her wrong, but she's alright. Her mama, her sister, and the beer joint welcome her maybe-pregnant-self back even though her jeans are bit more snug than before.

She Let Herself Go . . . . George Strait

She's onto a more interesting and exciting life, and she's looking damn pretty. Now it's her turn for an adventure, and she's leaving "tired of being tired" behind.

Husbands and Wives . . . . Roger Miller

Miller sums up rather simply and beautifully why so many marriages end up breaking apart—too much pride and an unwillingness to forgive. A smooth Nashville Sound arrangement that features a bouzouki solo, adding a Greek flavor to this standard.

Too Gone, Too Long . . . . Randy Travis

When she leaves him for good, he goes out and finds a new, true woman. She comes back begging, but she's an excuse short and a day late. A sad reminder of regret dressed-up in a feel-good, toe-tapping song.

You Look So Good in Love . . . . George Strait

A man grows bored with his woman, then rediscovers her beauty when he sees her out flirting with another. Strait frequents "you make me regret the 'Big D'" territory often, and here it's with a heavy dose of sentiment.

She Didn't Have Time . . . . Terri Clark

Her husband walks out and leaves her with their baby. There's no time to feel sorry for herself, to cry, to find love, or even to run from it. Thank God for flat tires.

HOW WE FEEL

I'm Movin' On .... Hank Snow

It's all over now, and this man needs a train and a truck to take him far away from his no-good woman. The more miles between them, and the faster he can go, the better.

Too Cold at Home .... Mark Chesnutt

Why do men cheat? In this story, it's because there's no other recreation available.

Have a Nice Rest of Your Life .... Randy Travis

Is it sincerity, sarcasm, or a mixture of both? With little left to do but accept the reality before him, this man decides it's better to wish his lover well on her way out the door than to curse her—a goodbye to remind her of all that she's leaving behind.

If We're Not Back in Love by Monday .... Merle Haggard

A husband pleads for one last get-away weekend. If two days of passion can't save their marriage, nothing will.

After the Fire Is Gone. .... Conway Twitty

The ashes of love are cold, cold, cold. Loretta and Conway play two lovers from two dying marriages who meet up to stoke what's burned out at home.

51 Surreal

"What the f@#k happened?" In a profound sense, these songs of the surreal convey the understanding that life is often strange and unexplainable. Stories from the front of country fantasy and myth, these songs are both rational and divine footnotes that make you realize that you just can't explain life.

Ghost Riders in the Sky . . . . Marty Robbins

A well-covered standard from the unofficial book of cowboy mythology, this song blends frontier folklore with Native American spirituality. Delivered here by one of the masters of cowboy songs, among other forms.

Highway Man. . . . . The Highwaymen

This Highwaymen theme song immortalizes Country's rambler myth, describing a shape-shifter with a transcendental knack for survival, and a job description that includes time-traveler and space explorer. The Highwayman as superhero.

Footprints in the Snow. Jimmy Martin

Often mistaken for a murder ballad, this bluegrass standard relates the story of the mysterious and unexpected death of a young woman. The strength of the song rests in its poetic observations and lyrical perspective.

You Can't Roller Skate in a Buffalo Herd. . . . . . . Roger Miller

What the heck's a "baseball pool?" Among other, even stranger examples, Miller uses his uncanny humor and the surreal to remind us that there's much in life we can't control or explain. Happiness, however, is always a choice away.

Call the Lamas!. . . . . Marshall Chapman

Chapman meets Buddha in a grocery store.

Sabu . . . . John Prine

Prine has a particular affinity for the unusual, as evidenced in this precious song about a childhood actor from India who finds himself a million miles away from home. To be exact, he finds himself on a dead-of-winter promotional tour in a Minnesota mall.

MY COUNTRY ROOTS

Wendell Gee . . . . .R. E. M.

No matter how much success these rock 'n' roll superstars garner, they never forget their Athens, Georgia Country roots. Here, an inspirational, if opaque, song about what else? A dream.

Wildfire . . . . Michael Martin Murphy

Where innocent dreams collide with dark reality, this tale deals a crushing blow to any child's dream of owning that ever-elusive pony. When this girl's horse breaks stall and disappears into a Nebraska snowstorm, she chases after it and never returns.

Rainbow at Midnight . . . . .Ernest Tubb

Sailing home to his woman after having survived a brutal war, this soldier has a vision that's difficult to explain, but easy to endure, as he puts the horror of battle behind him. The dream he has is about to become a reality.

Bears . . . . Lyle Lovett

Lovett uses his lyrical mastery to tackle and embrace the bear. He humanizes the animal that people tend to vilify and misunderstand. After all, he's a bear, and bear's need love, too.

Little Girl and the Dreadful Snake . . . . . .The Stanley Brothers

A walk into the wild proves fatal. In this surreal morality-tale that recalls the loss of innocence in the Garden of Eden, a father experiences his worst nightmare: losing a daughter.

I Don't Believe You've Met My Baby . . . . Dolly Parton

In this hard-to-follow dream-song, the singer's heart sinks at the sight of her lover with another, until she finds out in a case of mistaken identity that the mistress is just his sister. What a relief.

Seven Spanish Angels . . . . Ray Charles & Willie Nelson

An elemental tale from the frontier somewhere between Texas and heaven. Delivered as a larger-than-life booming ballad, this song involves love and rifles, in "Valley of the Gun" which maybe a cryptic allusion to suicide.

52 Country Is Identity

This list explores all sides of what it means to be Country as it relates to class, region and morality. If you identify, you belong.

Country Is . . . . **Tom T. Hall**

Are you Country? Take this test and find out. Hall provides a detailed list of requirements that includes thinking your own thoughts and loving your hometown. If you haven't done seventy-five percent of the things listed in this song, you're probably not Country.

Country Boy. . . . . **Johnny Cash**

A poor boy is free and able. There's the hunting, the fishing, and the all-important comparison between a country friend and a city friend.

Country Boy. . . . . **Little Jimmy Dickens**

Different altogether from Cash's version, this swinging song describes what it meant to be raised country in the 1930s and 1940s.

Johnny B. Goode. . . . . **Chuck Berry**

Country values intelligence over education. This musical legend got his schooling in the back-woods of Louisiana. He might not be a mathemetician, but he's the best guitar player around. A familiar story for many a Country musician.

Long Haired Country Boy . . . . **Charlie Daniels**

Some Country folk and some hippies aren't that different—they both like to get drunk *and* stoned. They may be poor, but they're content; they get high, but they're self-reliant. Back off.

Rock My World (Little Country Girl). . . . . **Brooks & Dunn**

The details in this song delight. A Camero-driving woman who acts like Madonna but listens to Merle blasts "Johnny B. Goode" as she rolls around town in her fancy boots, jeans, and jewels. She did well in school without opening a book, oh, and she can dance too! A girl who knows what she wants can wear a man out.

When Country Wasn't Cool . . . . **Barbara Mandrell**

While most were listening to the Beatles, the Supremes, or Marvin Gaye, others were listening to George Jones and drinking salty coke.

Country Club .... Travis Tritt

This song draws a stark dividing line between white "haves" and "have-nots." "County club folk" versus "country club members" replaces the dichotomy of city people versus Country folk.

You're Looking at Country................... Loretta Lynn

Country folk enjoy sex with their love, too, as long as it is preceded by a wedding band and a man who's not afraid to use his hands. This Country woman has always known exactly what she wants, and she gets it, too.

All American Country Boy .... Alan Jackson

In this telecaster-guitar-driven anthem of red-neck, blue-collar truth, you earn what you own. You're proud, partisan, and free. The shadow of being a member of a marginalized class is evident in the heart-worn pride.

A Country Boy Can Survive .... Hank Williams, Jr.

He may be down, but he's not dead. Radically self-reliant, country boys fish, grow, or shoot what they need to keep from starving. They're not afraid of much, including hard work, bad men, or other people's opinions.

53 Haunted

This list is dedicated to all the old lovers who just never seem to go away. From expressions of hate and spite to naïve romanticism, these songs span the territory where myth-making, memory, and love intersect.

I Can't Help It if I'm Still in Love With You . . . . Hank Williams

A classic Country anthem for mourning love lost. Earnest and moaning blue, Hank pleas with his lover, not so much to try and win her back, but as to explain why he feels so tortured.

Faded Love . . . . Bob Wills

The immortal father of Texas Swing, Bob Wills wrote the lyrics of this song to an old fiddle tune he heard his family play at home. The most melancholy bit of this story is that the speaker's recognition that love had only just started to bloom.

Do Memories Haunt You . . . . Hazel Dickens

Floating a unique mountain melody over a trotting bluegrass waltz, Hazel Dickens wonders if the same sweet memories that haunt her mind haunt his, too.

I Can't Stop Loving You . . . . Don Gibson

This classic, made popular by Ray Charles's 1962 hit rendition from his crossover album *Modern Sounds in Country and Western Music*, has conjured the memory of many a lost-lover, and been cut by everyone from Ella to Elvis.

I Just Can't Get Her Out of My Mind . . . . Johnny Rodriguez

A 1974 hit for Rodriguez, this song expresses the anguish and psychological torture of being haunted by the memory of love lost.

My First Lover . . . . Gillian Welch

In this gut-strung tribute to adolescent love, Welch meditates on a memory she not so much loves or hates, but can't forget.

If She Were You . . . . John Prine

Convoluted, yet sincere, a man taunts the women who left him by telling her about the women he has.

MY COUNTRY ROOTS

I Still Miss Someone . . . .**Johnny Cash**

Anyone who once had somebody has had the experience of watching happy lovers stroll by and revel in romance. Sometimes all it takes to raise an old ghost is the sight of other people in love.

Still My Thoughts Go
Back to You. . . . .**Jody Stecher & Kate Brislin**

Kate Brislin and Jody Stecher sing and play mountain music with the best of them, but their mountains are those of the Pacific Northwest, not Appalachia. In this gorgeous song, loneliness soars on the high lonesome harmonies back towards old love.

My Old Pal. . . . .**Jimmie Rodgers**

A founding father of Country, "The Singing Brakeman" yodels his way through the memories of his old flame, reminding us here now that no love compares to the love we miss.

I Miss My Mary. . . . .**Hal Ketchum**

The combination of Ketchum's smooth, hopeful voice and tasty, albeit traditional, production chops will have your dancing feet fighting with your tears.

Forgiving You Was Easy. **Willie Nelson**

Having found a way to forgive the woman who's done him so wrong, Nelson names the larger problem.

When I Stop Dreaming . . . . **Jim and Jesse**

No duo conjured haunted spirits like the Louvin Brothers and these Virginia siblings. Jim & Jesse capture the Louvins' arresting harmonies in a rendition of their mentors' original. Neither generation is getting over the past.

If I Talk to Him . . . . **Connie Smith**

A Queen of Country from the mid-sixties through the seventies, Smith pleads in this classic for someone to take a message to him. She knows that if she hears his voice, she'll take him back in.

54 Last Call

Whether you're ready or not, accepting that every great beginning must have an end is an important theme in Country and life. Here are the songs that both celebrate and lament the last call.

The Party's Over . . . . Willie Nelson

What would normally be a tough idea to swallow is made easier by the fact that tomorrow night holds another party. Oh to be Willie!

Closing Time . . . . Lyle Lovett

One of Lovett's defining characteristic as a songwriter is his simplicity. This song finds a performer at the end of a long evening, paying homage to those who pour the beer, sweep the floors, mix the sound, and at times, are the only friends a singer on the road has.

Young Man's Town . . . . Vince Gill

Usually "last call" refers to one more beer and an impatient bartender, but here Gill refers to another last chance that doesn't happen at night, but when you wake up one morning. It's not a hangover, but the realization that you are over the hill and time has passed you by.

Way Too Early to Go Home Now. BR549

Last call? This party just got started. There are times when you're just not ready to go home. These honky tonkers provide a spirited response to the bartender's dreaded last words.

I Can't Go Home Like This . . . . Ray Price

It's two-thirty in the morning again, you've had fourteen drinks too many, and chances are your wife will be waiting for your sorry self when you get home. Stylistically, this song evokes the Hank Snow classic "I'm Moving On."

A Good Time Was Had By All . . . . Porter Wagoner

Porter celebrates his old-time mountain roots on this knee-slapping ode to a big-night-out square-dancing to a band and caller. The song puts you on the dance floor, and in the middle of all the fun.

Journey's End . . . . Ernest Tubb

As this man approaches the end of a long life, he can't help but remember the woman who broke his heart. With the standard honky tonk bar band backing him up, Tubb captures the picture of a bar shutting down for the night. His last call is this last love letter.

MY COUNTRY ROOTS

Long Goodnight . . . . **Scott Miller**

Tonight will again be a long and lonely one. The goodbye he served his lover many years ago just won't stop haunting him. Sometimes the last call is the longest and hardest one to endure.

Waiting Around to Die . . . . **Townes Van Zandt**

Burdened by the weight of his own mortality, and the long slog of life, the character in this Van Zandt masterpiece spends a life trying to run away from his fears, but finds that the last call of death is truly inescapable.

I Dream a Highway . . . . **Gillian Welch**

In the spirit of the poets William Butler Yeats or Lord Byron, Welch pens this ode to life, legend, the road, and the spirit of Country. With a tried patience and delicate voice, she raises all of Country to the great unknown and blesses all with the hope of a never ending life.

Goodnight Irene . . . . **Johnny Cash**

The perfect nightcap. This recording, made at the Sun Studios in Memphis very early in Cash's career, is simple and well suited for any end. It is the sweetest "last call," the lullaby.

Where We Come From & Where We Long to Go

Country is characterized by a strong sense of place, particularly the places of our origins, the places we find or make sacred, and the places we long to go. Destinations are both real and imagined. The many roads we travel to achieve our destination, and the places we start from are abiding concerns in Country. Home, as place of origin, and everything that surrounds and defines home, has inspired many a Country song. Whether they are specific locations on a map, or universal metaphors that represent the landmarks that guide and define our long journey, here we find the geographic, historical, and cultural places that define our sense of where we come from and where we long to go. As the refrain of the immortal "Cotton Eyed Joe" suggests, "Where'd you come from, where'd you go? Where'd you come from, Cotton Eyed Joe?," location is significant, particularly to a music form with a "place" name.

55 Home

It is an irony of Country that a genre known for it songs about rambling is also known for the songs about the love for the place we rambled from—home.

Good Old Boys Like Me . . . . Don Williams

Listening to Don Williams sing is akin to sitting with an old friend and a fresh pot of coffee. He is paternal, unpretentious, and honest as a mule is stubborn. His love for his southern home is prideful in the least assuming ways. His ability to convey legendary writer Bob McDill's imagery makes this one of the truly great Country songs.

The Rains Came Down . . . . Steve Earle

....Upon the place where the ghosts of your ancestors reside, the land on which you have made your life, this is home.

Precious Memories . . . . Bill Monroe

....Of mother and father, of home, and a compassionate God to watch over it all—their spirits carried on the wings of soaring bluegrass harmonies.

MY COUNTRY ROOTS

I'm On My Way Back to the Old Home . . . . **Gillian Welch**

A place associated with childhood and innocence, home is a territory left behind. As time passes on, the details may change, but home always feels the same.

The Road Home . . . . **Travis Tritt**

Just as important as home is the path that leads you there. Often in life, as we grow older, so too does the road back home. Tritt mixes just the right amount of grit into his delivery in this, one of his best tracks.

Detroit City . . . . **Pam Tillis**

Unlike Bobby Bare's classic recording of this song, Tillis's version is fragile and extremely introspective. It serves as a perfect example of how the interpretation of a song can change depending on the delivery of the lyrics.

Blue Ridge Cabin Home . . . . **Earl Scruggs**

A place we wish to return as we approach our final days, completing the family circle in life and in death—the ultimate return to our Country roots.

Souvenirs . . . . **John Prine**

A warm eulogy to what we've lost as we've grown older. Graveyards and pawnshops not only rob us of treasures, but also our memories.

Old Blue Chair . . . . **Kenny Chesney**

Sometimes home is a chair set out in the surf.

Home Is Where You Are Happy . . . . **Willie Nelson**

Home is a state of mind. More than just walls and windows, it's about the people you share it with.

Home Grown Tomatoes . . . . **Guy Clark**

Nothing tastes better than homegrown. Sometime in March, you put the plants in the ground, and by August you are devouring tomato sandwiches—a favorite culinary staple of Country. Sometimes you don't have to travel to return home. Sometimes all you have to do is take a bite.

56 Hometown

Our hometown is where we're born, raised, and rooted. It's the streets, the people, and the stories that follow us when we leave—if we ever do—and it's the place that greets us on our return.

Our Town . . . . Iris Dement

Dement drives you slowly down main street for a tour of the town she's leaving, watching her memories roll by as the sun begins to set. This is a gorgeous portrait that makes you feel like her town is your own.

Hicktown . . . . Tennessee Ernie Ford

A filling station, a burned out movie theater, and a train that passes through once a day without stopping are a few of the attractions in this town, where every baby born and every person that dies makes a difference. It's like Mayberry.

Small Town Saturday Night . . . . Hal Ketchum

Same movie theater, same filling station, but now we're racing down country back roads, flirting, fighting, and living like there's no tomorrow. A feel-good song written by Pat Alger that captures the spirit of teenage innocence and what it means to rage against the night.

My Town. . . . . Montgomery Gentry

Where front yards are show rooms for old cars and tractors, where people still raise and lower the flag each day with deference, a hometown is something you share because you believe in it.

My Hometown Boy . . . . Marie Osmond

He is an obscure object of desire that her heart can't let go of—the one who sees the Country in this city girl.

Someday . . . . Steve Earle

A hometown can be a place you escape, if you're lucky, adventurous, or desperate enough to just get in the car and drive away. Earle's gutsy, signature delivery gives you the feeling that he made it out.

Take Me Home Country Roads. . . . . John Denver

Rural roads are the arteries that lead back to home as heart. When literal roads aren't available, Denver's memories provide the ticket home he desires. A great American anthem.

Welcome Back . . . . .Mike Ireland

This casually ironic song isn't so much concerned with the details of home as it is with the feelings of coming home.

Texas in My Rearview Mirror. . . . . .Mac Davis

A wild young Texan believes he won't survive if he stays in Lubbock, so he flees to pursue his dreams in Hollywood. Years of hard-luck pile up and turn him back to the warm embrace of his hometown. Hometowns are both for leaving and returning.

Readin', Rightin', Rt. 23 . . . . Dwight Yoakam

Yoakam captures the conflict between mountain morality and the industrialized South. When a family flees home for the promise of better wages, they're left with broken dreams and the harsh reality that their humble home back up the holler provided more. Yoakam at his best.

57 Mountains & Rivers

Mountains and rivers are significant geographical elements in Country. Symbolically, mountaintops are pinnacle experiences and existential burdens, whereas rivers are places of change, transgression, travel, and time.

Sitting on Top of the World . . . . .Clarence Ashley & Doc Watson

Originally a Country blues, this lyric celebrates perseverance in a time of loss. Adapted by many bluegrass and western swing bands in the forties and fifties, today it is a standard in both genres.

Mountain Music . . . . Alabama

Eighties redneck rock 'n' roll in its truest form. Complete with the broken down, hand-clapping chorus at the end, this song pays homage to the music of the river and the mountain.

Bury Me . . . . Dwight Yoakam

A person's last wish is to be laid to rest in the rolling, coal mining hills of Kentucky along the banks of the Big Sandy River.

Watching the River Go By . . . . .John Hartford

What could be nicer than sitting on your front porch, nude, with your neighbor, who is also nude, listening to the river roll by? Okay, it's a little strange, but strange is Hartford's thing. This song, recorded at the end of his life, mixes humor and endearment in a life-affirming way.

High on a Mountain . . . . .Loretta Lynn

Recorded when she was sixty-nine years old, this spirited, gut-bucket, broken-down song is really a chant. Loretta sings about the fond mountain memories of growing up in Butcher Holler, Kentucky.

Wolverton Mountain. . . . . Claude King

A ballad about a man's determination to marry the daughter of a dangerous, knife-toting mountain man. Based on a true story, this song was number #1 on the Billboard Country charts for nine weeks in 1962.

The River . . . . Garth Brooks

A song about the river of life and the choices we each make to ensure that, in the end, we can dock our vessel safely on a brighter shore.

MY COUNTRY ROOTS

Going Up on the Mountain . . . . **Jody Stecher**

A fine example of west coast bluegrass during the folk renaissance. The mountain, in this instance, is a metaphor for faith. Great bass harmonies.

You Gave Me a Mountain . . . . **Marty Robbins**

Robbins's vocals on the chorus of this track stretch out in grief as he describes a man at the end of the line, both emotionally and physically.

Chattahoochee . . . . **Alan Jackson**

This 1993 summertime song fondly reminisces about those hot Georgia days of adolescence spent waterskiing and French kissing girls, even though you didn't really know what you were doing.

Blue Ridge Mountains . . . . **Townes Van Zandt**

A man, void of redemption, offers this ode to the only place that he feels comfortable. Van Zandt most probably adapted this from earlier folk songs bearing a similar tune.

Tennessee Mountain Home . . . . **Dolly Parton**

There is nothing quite as beautiful as a clear spring morning in the mountains of eastern Tennessee, the place Dolly calls home.

High on a Mountain Top . . . . **Marty Stuart**

Again, the existential "mountain" of introspection is examined in this bluegrass standard. In his version, Stuart leaves the acoustic instruments at home and opts for a whiskey-tinged and hell bound sound.

Big River . . . . **Johnny Cash**

A Cash classic. A lonesome lover follows his girl down the Mississippi in hopes of winning back her heart, but realizes in the end that it's the river she's in love with.

58 Country Contrasted

Sometimes a statement of where you are *not* from adds dimension to a statement about where you *are* from.

We're Not the Jet Set . . . . George Jones

Other folks got big money and high culture. We got love.

Daddy Never Was the Cadillac Kind . . . . Confederate Railroad

For a man so plain, simple, and straight, a ride in a Cadillac hearse is an amusing hypocrisy he wouldn't have allowed in life.

Lifestyles of the Not So Rich and Famous . . . . Tracy Byrd

. . . are to be preferred. Who wouldn't want an RC cola and a moon pie over some dirty, salty, fish eggs?

The Money Tree . . . . Big Sandy & His Fly-Rite Boys

A Country swing tune about a man who's hoping his money will come from somewhere—ideally from a cash tree in the back yard. This is agricultural hardship versus entitled naivety, but tongue-in-cheek all the way.

The Coupon Song . . . . Bill Monroe

A young Monroe sings this morality tale about the risks of hoarding coupons. You can die the day you get rich. The best things in life are not in catalogue books.

Po' Folks . . . . Bill Anderson

Poor folks some times raise a great crop of kids, even when all their other crops fail. There's no greater wealth than love, which money can't buy.

Tramp on Your Street . . . . Billy Joe Shaver

No shoes on his feet, but he's free and knowing, wise and lyrical. Who needs shoes when you've got a friend—even if it is just for one night? A rare documentation of a young boy's first Hank Williams show.

I'm Gonna Be Somebody . . . . Travis Tritt

Some people are determined to close the gap between wealth and poverty.

MY COUNTRY ROOTS

White Trash with Money . . . . **Confederate Railroad**

Some people close the money gap but choose to maintain a cultural divide.

Don't Rise Above Your Razin' . . . . **Jack White & The Carter Sisters**

Humility, hard work, and honest living will bring you success. But don't let that go to your head, and whatever you do, don't leave the tribe.

Doublewide Paradise . . . . **Toby Keith**

One man's poor is another man's rich. When she leaves him all alone, he loses his sense of wealth, and begs her to come back and turn the frog into a prince again.

High Cotton . . . . **Alabama**

Poverty is no measure of true wealth. Sometimes when you think you're in the weeds, you're really in high cotton, and sometimes when you're in high cotton, you're really in the weeds.

59 Poverty

Economic status can also be a kind of geography.

Hard Times. . . . .**Tim O'Brien**

We sing to make things different and to feel better. We sing to celebrate the good in life, and to understand the bad. One of America's greatest songs written by one of it's first star songwriters, Stephen Foster. What it means to be poor.

Poor Man's House. . . . . **Patty Griffin**

A mother tells her child to lull herself to sleep by counting her ribs and praying to a God who watches over every last hungry soul. This is poverty embracing a family, and holding it up toward heaven—a touching song by one of America's premier singer-songwriters.

Jimmy Brown the Newsboy . . . .**Bill Monroe**

He, himself, is the news. Poverty sometimes wears the blameless face of a toiling, dutiful child. Plainly tragic, but strangely romantic, too.

Song of the South. . . . . **Alabama**

This song about Southern pride and Southern post-Depression history has a catchy chorus and, like many of Alabama's songs, it's best heard live with the audience singing along.

Coat of Many Colors. . . . . **Dolly Parton**

When poor is a state of mind, ideas can transform materials. A box of rags, a Bible story, and a loving mama can deconstruct the poverty mindset and re-make us as rich.

Busted . . . . **Ray Charles**

Quintessential Ray on this Harlan Howard blues song. He's broke, and all out of options, but don't feel sorry for him—just understand a desperate man can be dangerous. Simple defiance creates a kind of voodoo zen grace.

Patches . . . . **B.B. King & George Jones**

"Coat of Many Colors" for boys. B.B. and George provide powerful counterpoint to Clarence Carter's classic and less complicated version. There is a family reunion quality to the performance of this striking duet that claims the common culture of underclass black and white southerners. George singing the last chorus of the father's instructions to his son shivers the Country soul.

MY COUNTRY ROOTS

Mr. Poverty . . . . **Tony Rice**

This is a tricky song. It sounds so simple. But then there is this beautiful, intricate music, carved by poverty, twining around the words, creating the haunting knowledge that a poverty that is hard to endure creates enduring beauty.

Mississippi Cotton Picking Delta . . . . **Charley Pride**

This simple, almost campy song about growing up in the Delta is full of very complicated and dramatic imagery that conjure ghosts of Faulkner's literary landscape.

Hungry Eyes . . . . **Merle Haggard**

A boy watches his father watch his mother as she is ravaged by the deprivations of a Depression era labor camp. As the parents age into fear and sadness, the boy realizes for the very first time that he is of the lowest class. This is one of several Haggard songs that uses the Depression era as a backdrop for psychological exploration. Also on Mamas and Daddies.

60 Coffee, Cigarettes, and Sugar

Country is a culture of coffee, cigarettes, and sugar. Poor people's legal drugs are the staples of life that offer luxury in an otherwise deprived world. Here the staples of life become symbols of art.

Smoke Smoke Smoke . . . . Doc and Merle Watson

Swinging Texas-style in this smoking arrangement, Doc makes light of the fact that nicotine just might be the most addictive substance around. This chain-smoker's first words in heaven are, "who's gotta light?"

Don't Forget the Coffee Billy Joe . . . . Tom T. Hall

It is 1949, and a rural family lives on credit and the rabbits they shoot. Mama needs her medicine, and they all dream of store-bought coffee like some hope for gold and rainbows.

Instant Coffee Blues . . . . Guy Clark

A morning poem of regret after a night of making love. If it weren't for the cigarettes and coffee, albeit instant, you've got to wonder if they'd ever make it. Sometimes the worst things for you can provide the most sustenance.

Three Cigarettes in the Ashtray . . . . Patsy Cline

A simple, cinematic song about a woman and a man smoking and chatting away in a dreamy café—that is until another woman shows up and takes him away, leaving her alone with this image that burns in her mind.

One More Cup of Coffee. . . . . Bob Dylan

Essentially a Country song in spirit, featuring the gorgeous harmonies of Emmylou Harris. The only thing that can keep this young man warm after sleeping with his cold lover is another cup of Joe—then it's back down to an even colder reality.

Smoking Daddy . . . . Freakwater

This quintessential portrait of a chain smoker brought to you by this Kentucky-based duo contemplates the roll of the old "mortal dice" that's part of the Great Smoking Sweepstakes—not a contest you want to win.

MY COUNTRY ROOTS

Shake the Sugar Tree . . . . **Pam Tillis**

Since her man's grown older and colder, this woman's been deprived. Shake it out of him, or someone else, she's going to get her sugar.

Drinking from My Saucer . . . . **Bill Anderson**

Rooted in a Great Depression mentality, this spiritual song uses the metaphor of coffee as wealth. This man proclaims gratitude. Some people shout when they're excited, Anderson whispers.

Cigarettes and Coffee Blues . . . . **Marty Robbins**

Some people claim it's the best combination there is, but this guy would rather be in the arms of his lost lover than staying up all night, wired and chain-smoking. In a moment of pitiless empathy, he wonders how many others must be in his shoes. A classic example of the late 1950s, early 1960s "Nashville Sound."

Sugar Mountain . . . . **Neil Young**

Borrowing a page from the poet William Blake, this is Young's "Song of Innocence," an anthem to all things pre-adolescent and idealized. The mountain made of sugar provides the perfect antidote and escape from the reality of adulthood.

Chattanooga Sugar Babe . . . . **Johnny Cash**

Living in a hard-time, tough-luck world where nothing goes right, a man addresses his "Sugar Babe" in an attempt to seek sympathy and comfort. But she's got her own problems to deal with. Sometimes your sugar is also your salt. An old-time styled tune in the mold of "Froggy Went a Courtin'."

61 Roads

Road songs explore the peripatetic nature of man and life. The road is home, the road is bridge, the road is friend, and that's just the get-go.

On the Road Again . . . . Willie Nelson

Yes, Willie works way beyond the territory of metaphor. Here, traveling is a way of life, the pleasure of seeing things for the first, and maybe, only time—a kind of secular baptism coupled with the mature acceptance of loss. Still, there's the childish insistence that the road will bring good fortune as the place where willfulness is always gratified.

200 More Miles. . . . . Cowboy Junkies

A dry-eyed road song that accepts the price you pay to ride. Solitude, gossip, misinterpretation, and the loss of love while traveling towards realized ambition. When you've come so far, it's hard to believe you still have many miles to go.

Heavy Traffic Ahead . . . . Earl Scruggs

An early version of the road song narrative, this is a swing-blues, fueled by Scruggs's soulful banjo. Here the road is a musical journey with many friends and obstacles. Other recordings of note: Bill Monroe.

Red Dirt Road . . . . Brooks & Dunn

The road as a nostalgic path to heaven. Beer, Jesus, a shackled-up GTO, an old flame, and a wreck on the highway are all part of the revisited scenery.

Dirt Road . . . . Sawyer Brown

The Country equivalent of Easy Street, less the easy.

Don't This Road Look Rough and Rocky. . . . The Blue Sky Boys

For a nation of immigrants and enslaved people, a nation of people separated by vast distances from their loved ones, difficulties associated with travel are particularly poignant.

Avenues . . . . Whiskeytown

A wistful, yet detached meditation on the byways and highways that comprise the distances separating us from the ones we love.

MY COUNTRY ROOTS

Highway of Sorrow . . . . .Bill Monroe

The road as existential despair. When it treats you bad, it feels like it'll never end. This is one of several Monroe songs that utilize the road metaphor. The road life was no doubt a life he lived and knew well.

King of the Road. . . . . .Roger Miller

A carefree coronation for the rambler and itinerant laborer—a life on the road breeds familiarity and reinforces the hardships of being homeless. Maybe the most well-known and loved road song, it is certainly Miller's masterpiece.

The Moon & St. Christopher . . . . .Mary Chapin Carpenter

The road looks one way to the girl and another way altogether to the woman the girl becomes.

Highway 29 . . . . .Bruce Springsteen

This crooked road stops at a dead end: death.

Low Down Freedom. Waylon Jennings

Though the ostensible subject is still love, freedom, and change, here the road is an escape, not a source of knowledge. Written by Billy Joe Shaver.

Highway 40 Blues . . . . Ricky Skaggs

Ambition and dreams may take you away from your home, but the road is always there to bring you back. Skaggs's mandolin virtuosity is beautifully rendered in this song.

62 Motels

Motels and inns are "homes away from home" for the modern day rambler, outlaw, dealer, stray, or cheater. Ironic, surreal, or sincere, this list pays tribute to the lonely walls and tumbled-through beds of motel rooms, as well as the mystery and broken dreams they harbor.

Truck Stops Honky Tonks and Cheap Motels . . . . . . Byron Hill

The unholy trinity of a rambler's life, brought together in a perfect Country song about the *only* things that provide some predictability and comfort to a wayward life out on the road.

No Vacancy . . . . Glen Campbell

A gospel-swinging number, which shows Campbell showcasing his early bluegrass roots. The refrain is a metaphor for the alienation and disappointment that life continually deals the narrator of the song.

Motel Time Again . . . . .Johnny Paycheck

The character in this Paycheck hit is so drunk come closing time at the bar that he has no clue where he is. He heads for the nearest motel, where a number on a door lets him know he's home again.

Margie's at the Lincoln Park Inn . . . . Charlie Sizemore

The motel not only provides safe shelter for the traveler, but also for the cheater. This man's middle-American family life is a utopia, except for what his mind won't let him forget—the phone number and the friend he has waiting.

Sylvia Hotel . . . . Cheryl Wheeler

The name of this roadside inn sounds sweet, but no matter the sign, it's all the same: loneliness, memories, drinking, and another town to get to tomorrow. Someone should be cutting more of Wheeler's songs.

Tales from the Sad Hotel . . . . Jim Lauderdale

Here the Sad Hotel serves as a metaphor for life, which is, after all, only a temporary rental in between destinations.

Holiday Hotel. . . . . Loggins & Messina

The unsuspecting sideman in this tune accepts a job on the road playing guitar, and finds himself waking-up in exactly the kind of joint his wife warned him about. The title's innuendo should tell you that this is not your standard motor lodge.

MY COUNTRY ROOTS

Heartbreak Hotel . . . . **Conway Twitty**

Twitty shines in this version of the American classic that Elvis Pressley made famous. Here finger snaps tick off the moments to death giving a markedly more macabre tone to the observation that the bell boy and the desk clerk could work at a mortuary. The hotel is a waiting room for death—or maybe just an outer circle of hell.

Home Motel . . . . **Willie Nelson**

Apparently Willie knows about the Heartbreak Hotel, and he knows the address too—it's down on Lost Love Avenue, and he'll be there until she takes him back.

Motels and Memories . . . . **T.G. Sheppard**

A familiar story: She thinks her husband is out at another business meeting, but he's at the local motel having a different sort of meeting with one Mary Joe Jones. His memory won't lie.

This Hotel Room . . . . **Jimmy Buffett**

Written from the perspective of a guy's who's always gone and ready to get home.

Evangeline Hotel . . . . **Tom Russell**

The girl who comes to the big city to be a big star rents a room in this hotel, then realizes that every room is filled with broken dreams and broken dreamers. She decides it's better to just go home.

Okie Motels . . . . **Don Hughes**

This song is not about the kind of motel you find on the side of the road. It's about the kind of motel that rolls down the road—a house trailer, mobile home, or okie motel. Written from the perspective of a trucker, it describes the frustration and havoc okie motels can create for the big rig drivers out on the highway.

Cheap Motels . . . . **Southern Culture on the Skids**

These rockin' bastard children of Country capture the hard-driving feel of life on the road with only twenty bucks to your name.

Hotel California . . . . **The Eagles**

Arguably the most popular band to fuse rock 'n' roll with Country roots, The Eagles scored big with this hit about a man driving down the highway, looking for a place to rest. What he finds is a brothel that he can't escape.

63 Big City

A destination in contrast to the farm and the town, the "big city" is a place of destruction and the place where we go to discover what is significant in life—no matter how far away it may be. In Country, the big city is a setting far kinder to women than to men.

Streets of Baltimore . . . . .Gram Parsons

He sells the farm. They leave Tennessee. A country boy and a country girl come to the city and discover very different realties. A transformation begins. As the girl becomes powerful like the city, the boy becomes increasingly powerless, until he is forced to retreat alone to the safety of his rural home.

Jackson . . . . Johnny Cash & June Carter Cash

Jackson, the big city, the place where you go to strut your stuff, can also be the place where you are revealed to be less than you think you are. One of the great duets recorded by the first couple of Country.

The Fields Have Turned Brown . . . . .The Stanley Brothers

Abandoned things will die, especially when it comes to family. There is sometimes a high price for living and learning.

City Lights . . . . Ray Price

Promising to be the soul food for a broken heart, city lights often turn out to be a mask for misery. Noting that the stars were created by God, we are pressed to wonder if Price is suggesting that city lights don't have a very different origin.

Big City . . . . .Merle Haggard

An exhausting workplace, offering degrading, unprofitable labor is a place void of social promise. Sometimes the only thing you want to do is leave the city, but the city won't let you.

Pretty Girls, City Lights .Ralph Stanley & The Clinch Mountain Boys

Big cities are awkward, confusing, and impoverishing places for curious fun-loving boys.

City Girls . . . . .J.J. Cale

Beware. City girls vanish in the morning.

MY COUNTRY ROOTS

Lyin' Eyes . . . . The Eagles
...are city girl eyes, particularly rich city girls.

The Million Miles to the City . . . . Tom T. Hall
To the folks who live in small sweet towns, big cities can be
unimaginable and distant, as far away as youth from age.

Dallas . . . . Jimmie Dale Gilmore
The city has become like the woman. The transformation is complete.
Gilmore's nasal voice and quiet delivery make him one of the more
interesting singers in all of Country.

64 California

For some, California is the golden goal and for others, the place of many a grave disappointment. In Country, a reference to California has become a warning against devaluing where you are. Over and over, Country crooners translate Gertrude Stein's epigram, "When I got there, there was no there, there."

Do Re Mi . . . . Woody Guthrie

California has always been a land of broken dreams, even in the Dust Bowl days. This stereo recording is clean, crisp, and carried by the scream of a fiddle.

L.A. Freeway . . . . Guy Clark

Pack up this house and get me out of this damn town right now. These big city dreams have done nothing except cause me to value you more.

Southern California . . . . Tammy Wynette

A husband and wife can't seem to make it work. He wants to stay in Tennessee, but she has her gaze aimed toward the hills of Hollywood. A perfect example of countrypolitan music, both in style and subject matter.

Bloody Mary Morning . . . . Willie Nelson

Sometime last evening his girl left him. The only thing left to do is to get on a plane to Houston and see how many Bloody Marys it takes to erase her memory, or pass out.

California Cottonfields . . . . The Seldom Scene

An Oklahoma family sells the farm, loads the family on the Model T, and sets out towards the bright shores of the Golden state. A Steinbeck-esque tale of labor camps and broken dreams.

Marilyn Monroe/Neon and Waltzes . . . . Nanci Griffith

Hollywood's grandest and most beautiful fallen angel gets one more chance to cast her wink in this intelligent tribute.

All the Gold in California . . . . The Gatlin Brothers

This Country morality tale explores the risk of being an outsider in the ultimate insider community. Being a big star in Nashville isn't the same as being a big star in Beverly Hills.

MY COUNTRY ROOTS

Two More Bottles of Wine . . . . **Emmylou Harris**

For many, wine is a companion, something to put your feet up with and to share your trials and triumphs with, no matter the time of day. The fruits of California have healed and hurt many a willing soul in Country.

Good Time Charlie's Got the Blues . . . . **Waylon Jennings**

A resigned and broken man in an empty small town reflects on the migration of all his friends to the sunshine of California. This tragic, yet beautiful song is sung with remarkable tenderness on this track.

Heads Carolina, Tails California . . . . **Jo Dee Messina**

An upbeat, coming-of-age adventure story about two young lovers who flip a coin to decide their destination and destiny.

Barstow . . . . **Jay Farrar**

A postmodern analysis, told from the singer's point of view, about our consumer-driven world where cultural effects are left to gather dust or be consumed by a backhoe.

The Late Great Golden State . . . . **Dwight Yoakam**

An older man ponders the ramifications of panning for dreams in the golden state...you'll be fine as long as you leave your expectations at the border.

Going to the West . . . . **Kate Brislin & Jody Stecher**

Delicate harmonies and gentle guitar guide this sad conversation between a woman and her husband. She is going west to find a new life, but he is not.

If Hollywood Don't Need You . . . . **Don Williams**

A tender song about patience and devotion sung from the perspective of a small town man to his big city woman who, like many of us, believes her destiny and fame lies in sunny California.

65 The United State of Texas

Texas is another story all together. In the world of Country, Texas is America on steroids. Everything is bigger, meatier, and better. It is part of the South, but only in the way that Spain and Belgium are both a part of Europe. Whether it be the big lights and dollar bills of Dallas, the quiet plains of Amarillo, the dancehalls of Austin, or the intersection of Hispanic and American cultures on the streets of Laredo, Texas is a patchwork of tightly woven images which are always written about, and sung with, that unique Texas pride.

"T" for Texas . . . . Waylon Jennings

One of the cornerstones of the Texas canon, this live version captures Waylon bringing out the true grit of a low-down dirty woman that just don't treat this man right.

San Antone Rose . . . . Patsy Cline

Recorded by countless artists over time, the song, usually sung from the male perspective, mourns the memory of a love, true and fair, beneath the watchful eye of the moon and the Alamo. Other recordings of note: Bob Wills and the Texas Playboys.

Laredo . . . . Texas Tornados

A sub-genre of Country is tejano music, and like all tejano groups, this band, consisting of Freddy Fender, Doug Sahm and the great accordionist, Flaco Jimenez, delivers lush melodies that make even the most awkward men want to slow dance.

Don't Touch My Hat . . . . Lyle Lovett

Ask any man from Texas what his most important possession is, and more often than not, it goes by the name of Stetson and he wears it on his head.

Does Fort Worth Ever Cross Your Mind . . . . Keith Whitley

A heartfelt ballad about a cheating woman, the twin cities of Texas, and the limits of cold beer. Whitley, a Kentucky native, is one of the few non-natives that could capture the essence of Texas from up in Tennessee.

Amarillo . . . . Emmylou Harris

This poor woman has been working overtime to keep the women off her man. It's not good enough though, because he finally falls for a pinball machine and a jukebox. This is a perfect example of Country Rock at the peak of Harris's career.

MY COUNTRY ROOTS

My Hometown . . . . Charlie Robison

Drinking beer, smoking dope, playing high school football, and ending up in a Country band is what every Texas youngster aspires to, right? This smoky ode to Lone Star adolescence would have you thinking as much.

Miles and Miles of Texas . . . . Asleep at the Wheel

Swinging, bopping, and marching to the pull of a bow on fiddle strings, this song praises not just the size of the state, but the copious rewards that lie within its vast borders. Texas Swing to the "T."

Amarillo by Morning . . . . George Strait

A rodeo veteran ponders life on a trip from San Antonio to Amarillo. He may not have much, but he has the pride and comfort of being a Texan. Check out the version off Strait's live album if you think there is any question this is not a tried and true Texas anthem.

Northeast Texas Woman . . . . Jerry Jeff Walker

Written by Texas native, Willis Allan Ramsey, this serves as one of the best songs about the characteristics of the Texas woman. Who said Country music couldn't be laid back *and* funky?

Texas in My Soul . . . . Willie Nelson

Recorded very early in his career, this song just about captures it all. This is a very sweet and soft meditation on the state that contributes so much to American music.

Here I Am in Dallas . . . . Dallas Wayne

A broken man is forced out of Nashville by the woman who did him wrong. Since some say that Wayne is an under-respected and unappreciated musician, this song begs the question: Is the song about a girl or the music industry?

Ain't a Cow in Texas . . . . Dale Watson

Watson's humor is perfectly represented in this sarcastic song about false appearances. Two former lovers, each trying to goad the other into submission.

Luchenbach, Texas . . . . Waylon Jennings

Where do you go when you need solace and peace in the summertime? If you live in Texas, you go to Willie Nelson's picnic, held every year on the 4th of July. You don't feel any pain when you are in the midst of the red-headed stranger.

Texas Lullaby. . . . . David Allan Coe

For someone known as a hell-raiser and a drinker, the choice of this simple cowboy song might come as a surprise. Thinking about Texas can do that to even the most notorious and hard-edged performers.

MY COUNTRY ROOTS

66 Return South/Lost South

A return to Mother Dixie is a recurring theme in the Country canon.
When it appears, it is often presented with a co-existing exploration
of the theme of the Lost South. Whether or not true return is possible
remains an abiding question that is posed each day on Country radio
and in Country-stocked mp3 players, where contrasts between youthful
and matured impressions of the South abound.

Are the Good Times Really Over? . . . . **Merle Haggard**

Here, Haggard is deliberate and disappointed, a tone reflective of the
bitterness associated with a lost and glorious past. Some think our
country just isn't what it used to be. Classic Haggard.

Detroit City . . . . **Bobby Bare**

The big city has plenty of disappointment to dish out to anyone who
wants it. Exiled from the South, an assembly line worker in Michigan
pines for his home. This recording won Bare a Grammy in the early
1960s.

Highway Headed South. . . . . **The Whitstein Brothers**

After too much time in the frigid, frozen North, a Southerner returns to
sunny Dixie never to return there again. This contains beautiful brother-
style harmonies reminiscent of the Louvin Brothers.

Bright and Sunny South . . . . **Alison Krauss**

A twelve year-old boy leaves the bright and sunny South to fight in a
war. A modern power-bluegrass arrangement with traditionally rooted
lyrics.

Grandpa (Tell Me about the Good Old Days) . . . . **The Judds**

The stories we get from our grandparents allow us to understand where
we come from and who we really are.

The Night They Drove Old Dixie Down . . . . **The Band**

Narrated by a young civil war veteran, this song about the fall of the
southern empire is truly one of the greatest ballads ever written. Not
unlike the Confederacy, the Band experienced their own civil war,
which resulted in their break up in 1976.

Drive South . . . . **Suzy Bogguss**

All the answers to all our problems will appear. Just get in the car and
point it towards that Mason-Dixon Line. John Hiatt wrote this classic.

The New South . . . . .Hank Williams, Jr.

Known for his pugnacious Southern pride, Williams takes a more moderate stance here on the issue of Old South vs. New South. Things for the most part haven't changed, good or bad, except for the fact that the country boy married a Yankee.

The Front Porch Song. . . . . Robert Earl Keen

This song plays hide and seek with the South by meditating on a front porch. The porch was standing at the beginning and it will still be there after we are long gone. With the very last words of this song, Keen curses everyone who said the vanquished would not rise. Co-written with Lyle Lovett. He calls the song This Old Porch.

Sweet Home Alabama. . . . . .Lynard Skynard

Return to the land of youth, to kin, to the southland—without shame and without apologies, because the land itself, stretched out beneath those blue skies, is mother. And those we share the sky with are kin.

MY COUNTRY ROOTS

67 Music Row

Music Row, in the heart of Nashville, Tennessee, is the place where all the experiences from the farms, the towns and suburbs, as well as from the factories, coalmines, diners, and all the places that country people work, live, and play are transformed through a microphone into catalyzing stories.

Visit Me in Music City . . . . Bare Jr.

A sweetly cynical autobiographical rant-chant gives a rooted lay of the land in Music City. Bare, rather obviously, is the son of 1950s Country legend Bobby Bare.

16th Avenue . . . . Lacy J. Dalton

This song introduces the listener to the invisible heroes of Country music—the songwriters. They are the worker bees who produce the melodious honey we love so much.

The Pilgrim: Chapter 33 . . . . Kris Kristofferson

An elemental ode to the man Kristofferson was and the men he knew during his time in Nashville. It is a darker telling of the songwriter as hero tale.

Chasin' That Neon Rainbow . . . . Alan Jackson

He is back in the dream again. Let's hear it for the artist!

Baby Girl . . . . Sugarland

Girls play guitars too. This is a great example of what is being produced on Music Row right now—power-Country pop.

Nashville Cats . . . . Flatt & Scruggs

This tune celebrates the meticulous playing —"clean" —and deep passion—"wild as mountain dew"—of bluegrass pickers. There's sly sophistication, regional chauvinism, and implied profanity in this spicy little ditty that manages to come off sweet.

Nashville . . . . Todd Snider

Snider pushes against the bluegrass roots of Country. Surrounded by the hills that circle Nashville, he longs for the infusions of the blues blood (Jerry Lee Lewis) and Texas blood that are part of what gives Country its unique quality.

Nashville Blues . . . . **Doc Watson**

What would the music would be without blues and other infusions?

Guitar Town . . . . **Steve Earle**

Sometimes you just got to get out of town.

Me and Paul . . . . **Willie Nelson**

Nashville's hard. Ambitions, dreams, dreamers, money, hungers—Nashville has it all. Rumor has it, "Paul" refers to Tompall Glaser who, with Nelson, Waylon Jennings, and Jessi Colter, are considered the quintessential Folk- and- Rock-influenced Country outlaws.

Would You Catch a Fallen Star? . . . . **John Anderson**

It's a rags to riches town, and sometimes its rags to riches and back to rags.

Murder on Music Row . . . . **George Strait**

This song adopts the venerable form of the murder ballad, but in a nice ironic shift, analyzes the aesthetics of New Country. Written by underground bluegrass great, Larry Cordle.

MY COUNTRY ROOTS

68 Music Industry Songs

The music companies are the mines and factories of Nashville. These songs reflect the universal conflict between the need to self-express and the need to communicate to the masses—and the advertisers.

Don't You Think This Outlaw Bit . . . . Waylon Jennings

This song is Waylon's response to being arrested and thrown in jail during a 1977 recording session. He suggests that the authorities and powers-that-be profiled and then targeted him for claiming his "outlaw" status—a warning to those who think about going against the establishment.

Everything Is Free . . . . Gillian Welch

Our contemporary industry song, Welch sums up the vulnerability of being a musician who plays for love, not the money, in a time when too many people illegally download music for free.

The Man Who Could Have Played Bass in Sha Na Na . . . . Darrell Scott

One of Country's great contemporary songwriters, Darrell Scott weighs in with this song about a musician he meets who tells his story of broken dreams and regret.

My Home Ain't in the Hall of Fame . . . . Robert Earl Keen

This song shows just how much a writer/performer like Robert Earle Keen cares about the status and permanence that an establishment like the Country Music Hall of Fame has to offer.

F**k This Town . . . . Robbie Fulks

Fulks isn't saying anything that Cash or Waylon or Willie hadn't said before—this is his response to the proprietary exclusion of the Nashville Country establishment. This is a fun, biting tune you can all laugh and dance to. Not recommended for children, but definitely for those dreamers headed to Music City.

I Used to Be a Country Singer . . . . Gordon Lightfoot

When a singer-songwriter meets the woman cleaning his hotel room, he's moved by her tragic life story, which includes shattered dreams of becoming a Country music star.

Spokane Motel Blues............................Tom T. Hall

A Tom T. tune devoted to the thankless job of being a faceless writer in the Country music industry. Everybody else is playing in some better place, having a great time, and he's sitting in an anonymous motel room in some cold and rainy Pacific Northwest town.

Write Your Own Songs..... Waylon Jennings & Willie Nelson

The classic anti-establishment statement. An open letter in the battle between "The Outlaws" and the clean Country movement, Willie and Waylon make it clear who's generating all the profits in the music business, and if the suits don't like what they stand for, then they can go ahead and do it without them.

Outlaws Like Us ....Travis Tritt

Tritt's tribute to those before him and who waved the Outlaw Country flag. Despite the industry's unwillingness to accept or embrace their mythic status, the outlaws are still revered today as pioneers and legends in the industry.

You Never Even Call Me by My Name........David Allan Coe

Written by Chicago singer-songwriters Steve Goodman and John Prine, this song was made famous by David Allan Coe and is one of the greatest barroom sing-a-longs in all of Country.

MY COUNTRY ROOTS

69 Cities

Cities are places where some country folk actually live and dream, and where some others long to return to one day. Sometimes cities welcome you in and other times they spit you out—particularly if you're naïve or unprepared. These unique patches of Country's civic landscape seem to have a particular energy.

Lodi . . . . **Emmylou Harris**

Pronounced "low-die." A place you don't want to be, where the only way out is your own two feet. The place you are when everything goes wrong and you barely know where it is.

That's How I Got to Memphis . . . . **Tom T. Hall**

The heart determines the destination. A man follows the trail of his woman's tears, creating a trail of his along the way. He's walking the same road, running after someone running ahead on the road.

Cincinnati, Ohio . . . . **Connie Smith**

A woman walks halfway from Louisville, Kentucky to her home in Cincinnati, Ohio, where Heaven awaits across the Mason-Dixon line.

Kansas City . . . . **Brenda Lee**

Escape to fun—to Kansas City, the home of crazy lovers. The old blues men all do it, and little Miss Dynamite did it too. It's not a matter of how to get there, its a matter of when.

Is Anybody Goin' to San Antone . . . . **Charley Pride**

He needs a lift to somewhere, anywhere. Just drive him away from his memory of her. Other Recordings of Note: Texas Tornados.

Greenville . . . . **Lucinda Williams**

It's where old lovers go when they don't say what they mean, when somebody's always borrowing money and busting down doors, and you don't want to save or praise them anymore. Maybe somebody in Greenville does.

Houston . . . . **The Gatlin Brothers**

One day and six hundred miles away measures the distance between lovers—an eternity for some, but a relief for others that are happy to be getting closer to home and people they love.

North to Chicago . . . . **Hank Snow**

He's leaving, but wishes his former lady had a way to hold him home.

Crescent City . . . . **Emmylou Harris**

Nostalgia for New Orleans, the Crescent City, presented here as a place where grown folks play with their siblings all year long, all life long. Lucinda Williams, the reigning poet of place in modern Country, wrote this song.

Abilene . . . . **Waylon Jennings**

Abilene—it's pretty and it's sweet, and it doesn't treat you mean. Sounds like maybe he's really talking about somebody in Abilene (some Abigail or Amanda or Alice).

Going to Brownsville . . . . **Ry Cooder**

When the man who is rumored to have taught Keith Richards open G tuning takes a trip, a wise person rides along. There's always a reason to get out of town, and maybe it's always a good day when you decide to take the right hand road. This song may be about going back to someplace that matters before you die.

Ooh, Las Vegas . . . . **Gram Parsons**

A place you don't need to be, but love every minute of while you're there; a place where you loose so much you start to think you're going to win. Women, liquor, luck, and holiday inns where you never sleep comprise the kingdom that compromises this poor naïve boy.

Little Rock . . . . **Colin Raye**

The place where you go after you hit bottom and start trying to crawl out. The fragility and power of fresh born recovery and the seduction and treachery involved in brand new sobriety here described make this song memorable.

That Girl from Brownsville . . . . **Jim White**

If God will lie to a Brownsville girl for him, a man will become a religious fool for God. Then maybe God wouldn't be lying. See what the girls of Brownsville can do to a man?

MY COUNTRY ROOTS

70 Story Songs

Great story songs are jewels in the crown of the country canon. In this list we have leaned heavily toward songs where story is everything.

A Boy Named Sue . . . .**Johnny Cash**

A son encounters the father who abandoned him and gave him a girl's name and a tough future. Penned by the great Shel Silverstein.

Homecoming . . . . **Tom T. Hall**

A brief return home reveals the contradictions in a young musician's life.

I Met a Friend of Yours Today. . . . . **George Strait**

A chance meeting changes everything.

Dance Little Jean . . . .**The Nitty Gritty Dirt Band**

A little girl dances at her parents' wedding—and the band looses a bit of its cynicism.

Don't Take the Girl . . . . **Tim McGraw**

A boy moves from negotiating with his father, to negotiating with a robber, to negotiating with God—all over a girl.

Strawberry Wine. . . . . **Deana Carter**

A young woman chooses the season, place, and man, for her first big swig of love.

Ol' Red . . . .**Blake Shelton**

A prisoner, bent on escape, enlists the help of a bitch in heat. And, come to think of it, the way he sees it, a bitch in heat got him trouble in the first place. A modern day fable that explains how a certain breed of hound came to populate the South.

Six Days on the Road . . . . **David Dudley**

All the action is in the driver's mind. This song serves as a nice explanation as to why all those trucks on the highway drive like bats out of hell.

Last Gunfighter Ballad . . . . **Guy Clark**

An old gunfighter steps out into traffic.

Copperhead Road .... Steve Earle

A veteran, descended from moonshiners, becomes a marijuana farmer in this tale of Eden after the Fall.

If We Make it through December .... Merle Haggard

A not so sentimental Christmas story.

Harper Valley PTA .... Jeannie C. Riley

Momma takes on the local school board and wins.

Don't Take Your Guns to Town .... Johnny Cash

Cold and somber, this song is about a cowboy, a bit too green to call himself a gunman, who meets his match the first time he draws his gun. Mama's right again.

What We Believe In

First and foremost, that belief matters. Country embraces a patchwork belief system. Pride, love, family, friendship, hard work, truth, and Christianity are some of the bits and pieces stitched together to form the quilt of Country ideology—the day-by-day, sing-along-to-the-radio or iPod understanding of those aspects of life that are greater and better than any one of us. And Country theology is infused (largely through Celtic, African, and rural experiences) with an almost pagan appreciation of nature. Country belief is at once both secular and religious.

71 Spirit

Country transcendentalism, a philosophy that emphasizes both intuition and the divine, is steeped in a kind of Celtic farmer-naturalism, studded with an African sense of sacred place. These are just a few of the less conservatively Christian, but avowedly spiritual theologies, to be celebrated in songs belonging to the Country canon. There's more than one Unitarian Universalist church in Nashville and more than a few songwriters who attend. If he were alive today, Thoreau would listen to bluegrass.

Bright Morning Stars . . . . The Freight Hoppers

If only everyday could be started with this acapella, God-tinged meditation on that moment just before dawn, our daily gift of a new beginning. This North Carolina old time band hit the festival circuit in the 1990s as young traditionalists. You'd be lucky to catch a live show.

It's a Great Day to Be Alive . . . . Travis Tritt

We often forget, despite our gripes, that it is a gift to be alive.

I Don't Know Why . . . . Alison Krauss

A delicate and gentle cover written by Shawn Colvin, this song questions the questions that have no answers. We love and sing and protect because we need to, and that is good enough.

Cool Water. . . . . Eddie Dean

Recorded over and over, this song about a man, his mount, and the mirage that keeps playing tricks on them is a profound parable that leaves you thirsty.

Bluebird Wine . . . . **Rodney Crowell**

We've never had a sip of it, but if you got some, we'll surely try it. From the documentary *Heartworn Highways*, this is a live recording of Crowell sitting in a living room with his friends.

When in Rome . . . . **Nickel Creek**

A complex song that questions spirituality in this modern world of science and proven knowledge. One of the better examples of what might be termed postmodern bluegrass.

Hands on the Wheel . . . . **Willie Nelson**

There are moments in life when you look around and give thanks for, if nothing else, being in control, and in between the lines. Classic outlaw poetry.

I'm Not Afraid to Die . . . . **Gillian Welch**

Gillian Welch has the ability to take a depressing and complicated concept and turn it into an insightful and beautiful thought. This song about a hobo's last realization is a perfect example.

Waiting for the Sun to Shine . . . . **Lee Ann Womack**

There is a fine line between waiting around for something and wasting a good opportunity. Originally a number one hit for Ricky Skaggs in 1981, this version is heartbreakingly beautiful.

A Satisfied Mind . . . . **Jean Shepherd**

Recorded consistently across the genres of American music, this countrypolitan version is one of the few female takes on a song about having a positive outlook.

Let the Mystery Be . . . . **Iris Dement**

Some spend their whole lives trying to figure out life and death. Others prefer to sit back and watch it all appear and disappear. Dement's oddly twanged voice bends you through this Country secular psalm. Sister song to "I Don't Know Why."

It's a Big Ole Goofy World . . . . **John Prine**

In conclusion, when all the tears have been wept, the battles have been won or lost, and the bills have been paid or tucked back in at the bottom of the pile, it's a big old goofy planet we live on. As Prine often reminds us, levity is crucial.

WHAT WE BELIEVE IN

72 Family

In Country, family has traditionally meant *mama*, but recently, this has given way to daddy singing a whole lot about trying to be a mama. In the end though, its family—good or bad—whoever's doing what.

Mom and Dad's Waltz................................ Lefty Frizzell

Simpler times, simple love. Nothing is as simple, as complex, or as precious as Mom and Dad.

Daddy Frank .... Merle Haggard

Daddy is blind and mama can't hear; the children are well loved and don't recall ever having been hungry. This is a country family holding it together with music, industry, and determination.

There Goes My Life................................ Kenny Chesney

A man gets a girl pregnant. He sacrifices his dreams of adventure only to discover a new life with different adventures and adjusted dreams. This ballad is Country pop at its best. Chesney sings life into a subtly complex song.

No Charge .... Tammy Wynette

A mother, confronted with a bill from her child, responds with profound accounting. The kid scribbles, *paid in full*.

The Dollar .... Jamey Johnson

A mother tries to explain the economic "facts of life" to her son. In turn, she encounters the emotional facts of a boy's heart. Here, Freud trumps Marx.

Just Another Day in Paradise .... Phil Vassar

Instead of imagining heaven as home, now home is reimagined as heaven. The strange mis-adventures of one family, from curdled milk to sex interrupted by children, are lovingly credited for giving this life its holy quality.

My Front Porch Looking In .... Lonestar

Some people call this "The Sippie Cup Song," named for the popular kids cup. Instead of looking out at nature, this man is inspired by looking in at his wife and kids.

Mr. Mom. . . . . **Lonestar**

Mama's work is hard; still, some men are just finding this out. On some days, raising kids makes working at the office look like a vacation.

Easy's Getting Harder Everyday . . . .**Iris Dement**

There are babies and jobs, husbands and rain, but the flowers are dead and the music is far away. There is a thin line between safety and boredom.

Awful, Beautiful Life . . . . **Darryl Worley**

Life is tragic, but magic, if families hang together through the hard times. There's real risk and real pain, but somehow it is complicated and, oh, so beautiful.

The Good Stuff . . . .**Kenny Chesney**

A bartender explains what "the good stuff" really is—family.

Little Rock 'n' Roller . . . .**Steve Earle**

A father out on the road tries to be a dad from a telephone booth. While promising the distances will not always be between them, he entrusts his child to the care of his mother—and the angels that guard rock 'n' rollers.

Family Tradition . . . .**Hank Williams, Jr.**

Music runs in families; addictions run in families, too. We might look and act a little different, but, in the end, the apple doesn't fall too far from the tree.

73 Mama

Matriarchies abound in Country, along with those who would try
to overturn them. The power of mother is everywhere evident; it is
delicately and subtly praised from lyric to lyric.

Come to Jesus .... Mindy Smith

A mother tells her baby what to do when times get hard. She also tells
the baby that she will be waiting for her in heaven. Mama is always
there. Always.

Dear Old Mother .... Jim & Jesse

A poor country boy is able to write letters home because his mother
taught him to read. She calls. He responds that across time, and death,
that she and his father were once his only love.

Mama You Wanted to Be a Singer .... Elizabeth Cook

Mothers and daughters have mirror-eyes that see backwards and
forwards in time, eyes that see down roads not taken. Country music is
a country mama's little helper.

Memories of Mother .... Ralph Stanley & The Clinch Mountain Boys

A grass-covered grave suggests that the one who sleeps is forgotten.
Appearances can be deceiving. While mother receives her eternal
reward, her children plant flowers at her grave that will bloom each
new Spring, even when they are scattered everywhere far beyond her
protection.

Mamas Don't Let Your Babies Grow Up to Be Cowboys .... Willie Nelson

Mamas control the destiny of the women their sons will love, or at least
they try to.

Mama Don't Allow .... Doc & Merle Watson

Mamas don't have control over everything. This fun and rollicking song
shows that mama is intolerant of just about every type of instrument.

Motherless Child .... Blind Boys of Alabama

Wherever your mother is, is home.

Country Bumpkin .... Cal Smith

A tall, lanky, slow-drawling boy comes to town and meets a barroom girl with hard and knowing eyes. Country is mama loving the tiny country bumpkin nursing at her breast. Country is joyful tears and deathlike pain. It's waking up over and over to a glorious world of many wonders and looking forward to those yet to come. One of the sweetest songs in the Country canon.

The Baby .... Blake Shelton

What would a mama and a daddy be without one? This would be the psychoanalyst Winnicott's favorite Country song. Except the mama dies in this song.

In My Mother's Eyes .... Willie Nelson

Light and guidance, love and morality, fiction, creation, and money-making all begin in a mother's gaze of unselfish love. If this idea is in fact a reality, mother is where you find it. Willie doesn't sound absolutely sure it exists though.

I Had a Real Good Mother and Father .... Gillian Welch

Good parents go to heaven. According to Welch the children of good parents have a kind of prelude to heaven on earth, but they look forward to eternity with their parents on a brighter shore.

MY COUNTRY ROOTS

74 Kids

In the world of Country, kids are workers (as in "I Hope it Rains at My Funeral," "Ode to Bill Jo," "Patches") as well as benchmarks of achievement ("Something To Be Proud Of," "Hickory Holler's Tramp"), or failures ("Mama Tried"). They are also complex obligations requiring us to do everything from bribe the jailer ("Gallows Pole") to whore their older sister ("Fancy"). They are witnesses ("Carroll County Accident," "Mama's Hungry Eyes") and inspirations ("Country Bumpkin," "There Goes My Life"). The songs on this list are for kids, not about them— gifts of nature and magic for gifts of nature and magic. Let's have a sing-along.

Roly Poly . . . . Bob Wills and his Texas Playboys

He's the best-fed little boy in all of Texas. Twenty bread and jelly sandwiches a day satisfy only a fraction of this portly boy's appetite.

Jambalaya . . . . Hank Williams

This is not necessarily considered a children's song, but it is simple, culturally engaging, appropriate for children, and its Hank. There is a lot to learn and enjoy for kids in this song.

Froggie Went a Courtin . . . . Bob Dylan

The story of Froggie's marriage to the lovely Miss Mousey. Each verse introduces a new wedding guest until the old gray cat appears uninvited. What can you say? It was a short marriage.

Tennessee Stud . . . . The Nitty Gritty Dirt Band (with Doc Watson)

The most famous horse in all of Country music? He traveled far and near from Arkansas to Mexico and never threw his rider. This crisp recording captures the rhythm of the horse's gait.

Fox on the Run . . . . The Country Gentlemen

The chorus of this otherwise sad and woeful song is probably why this song is a summer camp standard.

Hopalong Peter . . . . Jerry Garcia & David Grismen

This traditional song tells of a goose playin' fiddle on a pumpkin vine and bow-legged rooster. The catchy chorus will have the whole family singing along.

Apples and Bananas . . . . .Keith Urban

The age-old song that exercises the pronunciation of each of the vowels. Who'd a ever thought Country singers could be elementary teachers too?

Sourwood Mountain . . . . Hobart Smith

This is one of the few instrumental songs listed in the book. Grab your kid, swing them around, and expose them to one of America's earliest musical genres, the fiddle tune.

Big Rock Candy Mountain . . . . .John Hartford

A hobo finds his own nirvana where there ain't no snow and you never have to change your socks. An alternative to Willy Wonka's chocolate factory for ramblers.

The Coo-Coo Bird . . . . Hobart Smith

This centuries old song uses the cuckoo bird as a metaphor for fickle and falsely motivated lovers. The song doesn't tell a story so much as it lays out philosophical statements.

Crawdad Song . . . . Clarence Ashley & Doc Watson

In the tradition of call and response songs, this fishing story examines cooperation and the pitfalls of greedy souls who take more than their sack can carry.

The Fox . . . . .Nickel Creek

A wonderful traditional tale, paced fast and furious in this version, about a fox that wanders onto a farm of ducks and geese one evening. The inevitable occurs.

Sneaky Snake . . . . Tom T. Hall

What is scarier than a root beer stealing snake? What's more humiliating than having your root beer stolen by a snake? Have you ever had a snake laugh at you?

Muskrat . . . . Doc Watson

This little-known river-swimmer has a nose for corn and trouble. He needs a shower, and he best leave this farmer's crop alone.

Little Birdie . . . . .The Cox Family

This song has deep and complex ramifications in so far that it is about lost love, but it still offers a great opportunity for a family sing-a-long on a road trip.

MY COUNTRY ROOTS

75 Friends

Friendships are platonic, yet passionate, alliances. Some of the sweetest love stories in the literature of the Country lyric are tales of friendship. Those who choose to companion and assist us without being tied by blood or a promise of sex have special value to those who lead hard and unpredictable lives. And so, it is not surprising that some of the saddest betrayals in Country are heard in the friendship songs.

Me and Paul . . . . Willie Nelson

In this song, Willie's friend is also colleague, a co-conspirator, and a co-creator of sanity on the road to staying sane and singular. Appearances can be deceiving, but you still might get thrown in jail because of the way you and your friend look.

Pancho and Lefty . . . . Townes Van Zandt

Friendship can be treacherous. An austere telling of the elemental tale of sons growing up, and into, a world they conquer and then are conquered by (all the while making friends and enemies) hangs on the events in the life of two drug dealers. One of the great songs, the Iliad and Odyssey of Country. Also on Outlaws/Bandits list.

Me & Bobby McGee . . . . Janis Joplin

Sometimes lovers can be friends. Sometimes. Contains a line for the ages that must be one of the most quoted lines in Country: "freedom's just another word for nothing left to lose." Kristofferson at his best, and that's sexy, articulate, and profound.

Tennessee Waltz. . . . . Roy Acuff

Music is his friend, a witness, a comforter—and a betrayer.

She's All I Got . . . . .Tracy Byrd

A friend can demand that a friend not do him wrong.

Good Bye Earl . . . . .Dixie Chicks

A friend will kill to protect a friend.

My Old Friend the Blues . . . . .Steve Earle

Got an old friend who always seems to show up just when you don't want them to? This friend is in a real bad mood.

Lean on Me . . . . **Rascal Flatts**

The R & B classic that became a summer camp standard (used to indoctrinate spoiled kids into the give and take of camaraderie) takes on a Southern accent in this live performance of the quintessential friend to friend-in-trouble invitation. This song is also perfect for a whole family in-car sing-along.

Highway Patrolman . . . . **Bruce Springsteen**

Sometimes a friend is a brother, but a friend who would abandon his brother is no friend. Yet another Country-tinged classic from Springsteen's *Nebraska*.

There's a Light Beyond These Woods
(Mary Margaret) . . . . **Nanci Griffith**

Friends stay up one night talking about what they're going to do, but end up talking all night about what they have done. A feminine take on friendship, ambition, alienation, romance, the work of music, and the call of motherhood that's "don't-stop-darling-beautiful."

Old Friends . . . . **Guy Clark**

Friendship as available and adequate. Time ripens friendships.

One of These Days . . . . **Neil Young**

This song is a sweet thank you note, a tribute to friends and unwritten letters.

Friends in Low Places . . . . **Garth Brooks**

As the legend goes—two fine songwriters were drinking in a bar not far from Music Row when they ran out of money before they ran out of thirst. One said, "I've got friends in low places," and headed off to find a few free drinks. The other started scribbling on a paper napkin. The rest is history. Garth Brooks recorded the classic version of this song—the Mark Chesnutt version is worth a listen, too. A song that celebrates friendship and commitment to lower class identity is elemental Country, deserving of many interpretations.

MY COUNTRY ROOTS

76 Married Love

We still believe in married love. That marriage is a powerful frame, a reviving sanctuary, a joy box, a love trough—is a specific and vivid concept in Country, where marriage enjoys a high pedestal that places it above less committed erotic alliances. This status stands in stark contrast to the presentations of marriage in rock, hip-hop, and blues.

We Go Together . . . . George Jones & Tammy Wynette

This upbeat tune about finding that perfect fit with your partner was most probably recorded by George and Tammy before D-I-V-O-R-C-E.

She Sews the World with Love . . . . Darrell Scott

A beautiful tribute to a wife who sews the blanket they sleep beneath each night.

Where Have You Been? . . . . Kathy Mattea

Sometimes we find the person of our dreams when we are at our wit's end with love. Sometimes we are lucky enough to spend the rest of our lives with that person.

I Flew Over Our House Last Night . . . . Tom T. Hall

A contemplative song about a man looking down from a plane 30,000 feet above the house and the wife he once had.

Eighteen Wheels and a Dozen Roses . . . . Kathy Mattea

This number one hit from the 1980s tells the story of a trucker who has a few more miles to go until his rig will be swapped for a Winnebago and a retirement with the woman he loves.

Louisiana Woman/Mississippi Man . . . . Conway Twitty & Loretta Lynn

One of the more famous duets from the 1970s about a love that required a fair amount of swimming in the alligator-infested waters of the Mississippi River.

I Got You . . . . Dwight Yoakam

You have unpaid bills and the car is out of gas. Creditors would be calling, but the phone is shut off. It don't mean a thing as long as you got your partner by your side.

She's No Lady .... Lyle Lovett

A questionably sardonic take on married life and the perceived role of the wife to the man. It takes on an ironic scent, given Lovett's former marriage to actress Julia Roberts.

Bring on the Night .... Alan Jackson

Sexy and smooth in a dimly-lit sort of way, like slow dancing in your living room with your partner while the kids are spending the night out with friends.

I'll Be Here in the Morning .... Townes Van Zandt

The sweetest gift one spouse can give to another is the promise that he or she will be there every waking morning.

The Bramble and the Rose................... Lynn Morris

A fortified marriage is protected by the strength of the commitment, just as the bloom of a rose is protected by the intertwining bramble. Other recordings of note: Jody Stecher and Kate Brislin.

Magnolia Wind .... Guy Clark

Even the most beautiful things in life lose their luster when you don't have a willing partner to share them with. Simple, sweet, and sung by a wizened soul.

77 Good Love

When the heart and the body and the soul are present, wedding rings and church vows and children can be irrelevant. This is good love. It is a soul-recognizing-soul commitment that might be more saliently explored in the roots of rock, hip-hop, and blues, but it exists in Country—and when it occurs, is all the more poignant, radical, and striking for going against the common grain.

I Walk the Line . . . . Johnny Cash

Commonly believed to be the song Johnny wrote for June, it defines the "straight and narrow life" that devotion demands of a partner. That classic slap-snare rhythm guitar sound on this track is a signature of the early Cash sound.

The Happiest Girl in the Whole U.S.A. . . . . Donna Fargo

Some mornings, you wake up next to a lover and everything is absolutely perfect. Here, a woman is overwhelmed with joy when good love transforms morning routine into a gift sent down from heaven above.

Deeper Than the Holler . . . . Randy Travis

There's a thousand songs that say "I love you," but there's only one way for this country boy to express the depth of his devotion for his lover: by saying it *his* way in a bass/baritone voice that made many a heart melt.

Save the Last Dance for Me . . . . Emmylou Harris

True love lives on a foundation of trust and faith, but sometimes it's necessary to remind the one who's far from home not to forget or betray the rock of love waiting at home.

Good Woman's Love . . . . Tony Rice

This Cy Coben song is a lost and found story about a troubled rambling man who is graced by the committed love of a tried-and-true woman— a dream every man hopes for and few are blessed to receive.

Flesh and Blood . . . . Johnny Cash

In this poetic ode to love and nature, Cash meditates on the spirit of his lover by intimately interacting with and observing the natural world. As powerful as the spirit he conjures is, it's the body he both longs for and needs.

Please Don't Tell Me How the Story Ends . . . . . **Ronnie Milsap**

Ronnie's voice at its best on this Kristofferson song about a man who wants to revel in the good love of the moment before jumping to the darker realities of the situation. No one sang the word "softer" more beautifully than he does here. This is Kristofferson's Buddhist offering to a one-night stand.

Watch the Wind Blow By . . . . **Tim McGraw**

This song, written by Anders Osborne, is one big ole' scoop of Country Soul. A man and a woman revel in and savor each kiss on the last summer night in autumn. In Country, good love is often influenced by the changing seasons.

You Asked Me To. . . . . **Billy Joe Shaver**

An essential part of good love is radical belief. You don't question your lover, you happily just do as they ask, no questions needed. A song Jennings wrote with Shaver, the unconditional lyric here resonates more fully when you consider the two outlaws who wrote it.

78 Loving Lies

Love and lies, lies and love. Sometimes one leads to the other, and sometimes one destroys the other. Lies, the destroyer of love, have their place in love—and that's a grown-up Country truth.

Gentle on My Mind . . . . Glen Campbell

The narrator takes pleasure in and is drawn to his woman precisely because she doesn't tie him down, hence he keeps his sleeping bag behind her couch. He's gone but he's coming back. And he's not sleeping with some other girl—he's out drinking coffee with hobos. Yeah, right.

Oh, Babe It Ain't No Lie . . . . Elizabeth Cotten

And sometimes when you love only one, some old gossip starts lying and saying that you are loving two. Or maybe she's telling the truth, and you are lying. Maybe you didn't just get home. Maybe you didn't bring all your money back with you. Anyway, this one is about love and lies.

Anyhow, I Love You. . . . . Guy Clark

And maybe even if he has lied about some things, he hasn't lied about anything important.

Paper Mansions . . . . .Dottie West

The familiar Country simile of heaven as mansion is here appropriated—and amended—to chide a lying lover.

Pitfall. . . . . The Louvin Brothers

Loving a lying woman is a fall into a dangerous hole. A particularly violent image to miners, oil well diggers, and any man who's ever had sex. Other recordings of note: The Whitstein Brothers.

It Only Hurts When I Cry. . . . . Dwight Yoakam

Tantalizing with his contradictions, Yoakam pronounces himself honest, except for the instances when he is dishonest, and then proceeds to tell another lie. This song juggles timeless images of teardrops and sunshine with references to recovery that are at once dated and timely.

Ocean Front Property. . . . . George Strait

The lover assumes the macho pose he thinks he needs to take to attract his woman, saying he can and will do without her if need be; then he signals that the posture is a vanishing mask.

Rock, Salt & Nails .... Buddy & Julie Miller

In this song, a lie is an excuse for gothic horror and revenge. Who ever wrote this song terrifies. Shame and conscience are mentioned, along with an inability to sleep. Borderline personality disorder? Socio-path? What's even more discombobulating is that this song is so gorgeous.

Makin' Believe .... Kitty Wells

Making believe when you can't make love. If the lies we tell ourselves are not the worst, they are surely the hardest to stop telling.

You Win Again......................... Conway Twitty

And sometimes we lie by believing someone's unbelievable truth. Recorded early in Twitty's career, this song has more of a doo-wop rock 'n' roll feel.

Alibis .... Tracy Lawrence

And sometimes, by our example we teach our sweethearts to lie. We then live to be deceived by liars who were taught by masters. Here, the cuckolded becomes a triple-threat cuckold.

MY COUNTRY ROOTS

79 Love and the Road

Love and "the road"—where two contradictory yet complimentary impulses combine, each providing an insight into the other. Nurture encounters adventure, as security encounters danger. Sometimes having one means giving up the other; but some songs suggest you can have your cake and eat it, too.

Wagon Wheel . . . . Old Crow Medicine Show

Originally a Bob Dylan composition, this ode to the highway and a woman in Raleigh is lyrically reinterpreted by these mountain music masters. Just try to listen and not sing along.

Windfall . . . . Son Volt

Driving down a state road in the middle of who-knows-where, late in the evening, listening to whatever the AM radio has to offer—for some there is no closer place to heaven. A great example of postmodern Country.

No Lonesome Tune . . . . Townes Van Zandt

Sometimes when we hit the road in search of something outside of ourselves, the only thing we discover is a deep longing for those we have left behind.

On and On . . . . .Bill Monroe

This lonesome highway bluegrass tune has an uplifting, "get-on-out-the-door" kind of feeling.

River Stay Away from My Door . . . . .Tex Williams

Just let a broken hearted man with nothing to show-for be. Leave him alone with his misery. Williams's bass vocal, combined with the flailing of the banjo, bounce this song to and fro.

Threadbare Gypsy Soul . . . . Pat Green

Borrowing from both the cowboy and bohemian schools of philosophy, this anthem captures just what exactly drives the wandering troubadour, at least in Texas.

Wait a Minute . . . . .The Seldom Scene

Written by the West Coast bluegrass great, Herb Pedersen, this song gently captures the tension musicians on the road feel with their loved ones back at home.

Every Time You Say Goodbye . . . . **Alison Krauss**

Listening to Kraus's angelic voice makes you wonder how any one could leave such a beautiful girl behind.

Highway of Sorrow . . . . **Bill Monroe**

I wouldn't recommend heading down this road: a cautionary tale to men about the potential futility of fooling around on a good woman.

She Went Out for Cigarettes . . . . **Chely Wright**

What began as a quick trip to the local mini-mart ended up being a journey that would change her life forever. Meanwhile, back at home, the game just went into halftime and he just realized she is no longer there.

The Road to Ensenada . . . . **Lyle Lovett**

A haunting number about a man and the road that took him to Mexico in hopes of forgetting his home and his family. Regretful, beautiful, and complex.

I Will Always Love You . . . . **Dolly Parton**

No matter where you are my heart is with you, for love has the greatest reach. One of the great love letters in all of American music, this song is delivered with care, tenderness, and sheer Parton power.

MY COUNTRY ROOTS

80 Mama Earth

Following the legacy of early European literary traditions, Country too celebrates nature—the material and the sensual—in pastoral odes to THE mama of us all—earth.

You Are My Flower . . . . Flatt and Scruggs

The most elemental and simple of all Country songs relating to fauna, this sweet love song was originally made popular by the Carter Family.

Acony Bell . . . . Gillian Welch

A gentle celebration of a little known wildflower found only the mountains of North Carolina and Georgia in early April—one of the most rare harbingers of spring.

A Poor Man's Roses (or a Rich Man's Gold) . . . . Patsy Cline

A woman is faced with a tough decision between her heart and her needs. Don't they say that flowers are the quickest way to a woman's heart?

The Blackest Crow . . . . Tim O'Brien

Penned in a style reminiscent of a Shakespearean sonnet or a Robert Browning poem, this traditional pledge of faith and loyalty to a departing love will bring a tear to your eye.

Wine Colored Roses . . . . George Jones

A hopeful and lonely woman phones up her ex to see if he is still a slave to the bottle. He sends her twelve wine-colored stems in an attempt to make saying "yes" a little easier.

Southwind of Summer . . . . The Flatlanders

This meditation on the inevitable, yet renovating, quality of the Texas breeze flows gently and gracefully from this Lone Star supergroup of super songwriters.

Hickory Wind. . . . . Gram Parsons

The natural elements of our youth and upbringing serve as a medicinal tonic to the way we experience the rest of our lives, good or bad. Such is the case with this South Carolina breeze. Other recordings of note: Emmylou Harris.

Willow Tree . . . . Tony Furtado

Singer Kelly Jo Phelps joins banjo virtuoso Furtado in this sparse, emotional ballad about death, the memory of those who have gone before us, and the tree most often associated with both.

Georgia Rose . . . . The Seldom Scene

A fast-paced bluegrass standard about a woman from the north Georgia hills. This version features one of the greatest examples of the high lonesome tenor, that being the voice of the late, great, John Duffey.

Light of a Clear Blue Morning . . . . Dolly Parton

This is a Dolly power ballad. It is a song which rejoices in the rejuvenating effect of new beginnings, specifically as the sun rises over the mountains of her east Tennessee home.

Sugar Magnolia . . . . The Grateful Dead

This psychedelic Country classic extols the groupie—she who follows, tends to, and acquiesces to, each and every demand of the band members.

Daisy a Day . . . . Wilma Lee Cooper

A touching song about a man who brings his lover a song and a daisy each day until she dies. He decides to do the same for her headstone.

High Sierra . . . . Emmylou Harris, Dolly Parton, and Linda Ronstadt

What happens when you match three of the biggest and most influential voices in Country music with a song that demands big, tight harmonies? Sit down when you listen to this track, because otherwise you might faint.

Wildwood Flower . . . . June Carter Cash

This nineteenth century ballad was passed down through four generations of the Carter Family before it was taught to June. A rare recording, most versions recorded within the last fifty years are instrumental.

MY COUNTRY ROOTS

81 History

In Country the immutable past provides a kind of certainty that can be solace. Singing history is one way of taking control of facts.

Ragged Old Flag . . . . .Johnny Cash

One man meets an older man in a town square and makes a comment about the town's "ragged old flag." The old man explains that the flag has seen a lot, and proceeds to give the younger man a beautiful history lesson.

Christmas in Washington. . . . . .Steve Earle

America is only as successful as the people who have stood up over time against tyranny and injustice and demanded change towards the inclusion of all its citizens. This ode to Woody Guthrie serves as a love letter to all of those who have fought the good fight of justice and liberty for all.

1913 Massacre . . . . Woody Guthrie

In 1913, in Calumet, Michigan, a company of miners and their families gathered to celebrate Christmas dinner with one another. At some point that night, a fire broke out, a stampede ensued, and seventy-three people ended up perishing. Guthrie claims, as did many others, that the company bosses maliciously yelled "fire!" When the investigators arrived they realized there had been no fire.

The Battle of New Orleans. . . . . Jimmy Driftwood

Despite the fact that a treaty had been signed two weeks earlier ending the war, the Battle of New Orleans went on as planned, due to the fact that word hadn't yet reached Louisiana. The Americans, under General Andrew Jackson, defeated the British with the help of Caribbean pirates.

The Wreck of the Edmund Fitzgerald . . . . Gordon Lightfoot

This ship's sinking remains the greatest disaster in Great Lakes maritime history. She was full of iron ore and on her way across Lake Superior when a storm approached. To this day nobody knows exactly what happened.

Ben McCullough . . . . .Steve Earle

This is a ballad written from the perspective of a foot soldier in the Texas army during the Civil War. In this telling of the tale, many more died of disease and of malnourishment than by bullets. This song investigates the many contradictions and confusions that typified the War between the States.

Mr. Garfield . . . . **Johnny Cash**

Less than four months after becoming the twentieth president of the United States, James Garfield was shot while catching a train. It is said that the president could have survived were it not for the inadequate medical care he received.

She Thinks His Name Was John . . . . **Reba McEntire**

Written in response to the AIDS scare that began to permeate the American landscape in the 1980s, this ballad relates the story of a deadly one-night stand.

Ruby Ridge . . . . **Peter Rowan**

In 1992 in Northern Idaho, the Bureau of Alcohol, Tobacco and Firearms opened fire on what they believed were Aryan sympathizers. In the exchange of fire, a wife of one of the suspects was shot dead while holding her newborn baby in her arms. After an investigation, the U.S. Government was censured and forced to pay a sizeable restitution.

Where Were You . . . . **Alan Jackson**

Written in response to the September 11, 2001 terrorist attacks in New York City and Washington D.C., this song pays tribute to those who lost their lives and attempts to comfort the rest of us. A 9/11 song that leaves the jingoism out.

John D. Lee . . . . **Jody Stecher & Kate Brislin**

Lee, a central figure in the establishment of the Mormon Church in Utah in the 1860s, was convicted for his part in what was called the "Mountain Meadows Massacre"—an alleged attack by Mormons on a party of pioneers. Lee was executed for his supposed part in the carnage, even though he believed he was following orders.

Ballad of the Alamo . . . . **Marty Robbins**

Men assembled from all over the South in an attempt to fortify the famous San Antonio bastion. In the end only 185 men were left to fight against the 5,000 men of Santa Anna's Mexican army. They fought until the end but lost their lives in the process.

The Ballad of Ira Hayes . . . . **Townes Van Zandt**

Ira Hayes, a Pima Indian known as "Falling Cloud," was one of the marines who took Mount Suribachi at the battle of Iwo Jima in World

War II. The raising of the American flag in this battle became one of the iconic images of the war. Upon his return to America, Hayes, unable to cope with his newfound celebrity, alongside the irony of being a freedom-fighter confined to a reservation, died in the depths of alcoholism.

Atomic Power . . . . **Uncle Tupelo**

A simple song about the most complex of situations that emanated out of the Cold War. There is a religiosity to this song that keeps it in the fold of traditional American music.

82 Irony

In the world of Country, contradictions are significant.

Act Naturally............................. **Buck Owens**

Sometimes it's the lie that tells the truth, and the truth that tells a lie. And sometimes what we see is what we get and people think it's an act. That's ironic. Buck Owens juxtaposes the sophisticated art of film against the simple art of song in a manner that suggests the superiority of song.

She Only Smokes When She Drinks ....**Joe Nichols**

When she looks available, she isn't.

She Thinks I Still Care..................... **George Jones**

And he thinks he doesn't. She knows his feelings better than he knows his own feelings.

Stand by Your Man......................... **Lyle Lovett**

Tammy's version is sincere, if pathetic. Lyle's version is acerbic and ironic.

God Will.................................... **Lyle Lovett**

God's love is used as an element for a heady put-down.

Do You Want Fries with That?................. **Tim McGraw**

A man who was once rich in possessions and in relationships ends up working the drive-through window at McDonalds, waiting on the man who took it all away.

When You Were Cheatin' .... **Gretchen Wilson**

The aftermath of infidelity is anything but glamorous.

He Thinks He'll Keep Her............**Mary Chapin Carpenter**

.....But she's really keeping him—until she decides to leave or stay. In the end, what he thinks doesn't really matter at all.

Holding Her and Loving You............**Earl Thomas Conley**

The irony here is that the cheating man thinks he's the victim.

Would You Catch a Falling Star ....**John Anderson**

The only star you can touch is one that has fallen from the sky.

WHAT WE BELIEVE IN

The Perfect Country and Western Song...... David Allan Coe

....isn't. This song (about song-construction formulas) self-consciously breaks more rules than it intends to—and that's part of the charm of its text. There is also the sly irony of constructing a song about the construction of songs in a genre that prides itself on simplicity.

The Grand Tour .... George Jones

Come on in. He would love to show you the house where it all went wrong. Over here are the bad memories and in this room is where she walked out on him. Isn't it lovely? Yet another George Jones classic.

83 Labor

Labor is either the badge of honor or the prison at the root of Country.
It is an understanding of hard work as religion, and then, perhaps
more profoundly, as a theology to be abandoned. With these songs,
Calvinistic doctrine is overthrown by a born-in-the-Bible-Belt-of-Music-
Row-washed-in-the-blood reminder: it is not by works or work that we
are saved.

Sixteen Tons . . . . Tennessee Ernie Ford

In this song, the laborer is stuck and just can't get ahead. Often,
desperate laborers would contractually agree to a payment of goods
from the company store, rather than cash. In the process, they lost their
self-determination.

Ode to Billy Joe. . . . . Sinead O'Connor

Far from the myth of moonlight and magnolias, this belle chops cotton
while her brothers bale hay, her father ploughs, and her mother cooks,
cleans, and washes. Bobbie Gentry paints an unerring portrait of a
striving Mississippi delta farm family, dulled both by their morning of
hard labor and by the anticipation of labor, they fail to notice their sister
having a breakdown at the table.

In Tall Buildings . . . . John Hartford

A sleepy, almost lullaby about the entrapment of offices and the
corporate life.

Peach Picking Time in Georgia. . . . . Jimmie Rodgers

The laboring calendar becomes the calendar of love.

Blue Collar Man . . . . Travis Tritt

Honoring those who bust their butts, sun up to sun down, five days a
week.

Whichita Lineman. . . . . Glen Campbell

A telephone lineman is an object of desire. Ever-present labor, ever-
present love.

Ain't Gonna Work Tomorrow . . . . Wilma Lee Cooper

There are commitments greater than the commitment to labor—those
made to love and to love lost. In other words, sometimes you just don't
go to work.

MY COUNTRY ROOTS

Workin' Man's Ph.D. . . . . .Aaron Tippin

Hard work, humility, and the satisfaction of a quality product are three of the requirements towards receiving a Ph.D. in America's labor force.

40 Hour Week . . . . Alabama

There is a shout out to autoworkers, steel mill workers, hammer swingers, nail drivers, counter help, firefighters, mailmen, factory workers, field workers, coalminers, big rig drivers, warehouse workers, waitresses, mechanics, and policemen in this late twentieth century valentine to labor.

Nine Pound Hammer. . . . . Merle Travis

Hard, hard work and relief and beer are too far away. A coal miner's life makes him feel small. He ends up wishing for big lump of coal tombstone.

Take this Job and Shove It . . . . .Johnny Paycheck

Rebellion from the tyranny of the factory is rather easy when one doesn't have a spouse for whom one wishes to provide. Outlaw punk at its finest from the anti-authoritarian Paycheck.

84 Simple Wisdom

We now enter the realm of Country self-help. Inspirational and instructive, sometimes simple-minded, but often useful, these wildly popular ditties are chock-full of simple wisdoms distilled from life by a people known for pulling themselves up by their own bootstraps.

I Hope You Dance . . . . **Lee Ann Womack**

Don't be a wallflower. A series of poetic wishes for a life vividly engaged. Perfect for graduations.

To Live Is to Fly. . . . . **Townes Van Zandt**

Thinking about the inevitable losses in life makes the loss no less inevitable or tragic. This is hard wisdom for the hard journey that is life: acknowledge the deficits, turn no opportunity away, fly low, fly high, but keep traveling. Keep waking up, keep shaking sorrow off, so you can keep traveling.

I Washed My Face in the Morning Dew . . . . **Tom T. Hall**

Cuddle close to God; touch nature. Revive and refresh yourself from the horrors of the man-made world by close encounters with that which man did not make.

Live Like You Were Dying . . . . **Tim McGraw**

Knowledge that death is coming frees one to live.

The Gambler . . . . **Kenny Rogers**

Something about "knowing" is being said in this Don Schlitz classic and something about engagement. In the midnight silence of this song that begins with the last drink of an aging gambler, there is a wisdom that makes a lot of people stop feeling sorry for themselves and start playing the game of life, regardless of the cards in their hand or the money on the table.

Mr. Gold and Mr. Mudd . . . . **Townes Van Zandt**

A retelling, with the help of a deck of cards, of the old Bible story about the last being first and the first being last, and Eve being at the center of things.

Mud on the Tires. . . . . **Brad Paisley**

What's with all the mud imagery? Embrace experience and the dirt it brings with it.

WHAT WE BELIEVE IN

Needless to Say . . . . **Loudon Wainwright III**

Life is difficult to explain, but sometimes good advice is enough to get you going. A good wish is a fine companion for those who try to welcome change.

Dust on the Bible . . . . **David Lee Murphy**

Age brings wisdom.

How Can I Help You Say Goodbye . . . . **Patty Loveless**

When confronting loss, the movement of time helps. Present love, even of a different kind, helps until time does its job.

We Don't Run. . . . . **Willie Nelson**

A prayer of sorts that asks for direction, patience, and love from the church of Mr. Nelson.

Don't Ask Me How I Know . . . . **Bobby Pinson**

You're going to make mistakes, and get some wisdom to call your own—if none of your mistakes are fatal, that is. This is a charming litany of the unacknowledged mistakes one man made, revealed by his commandments.

Come from the Heart . . . . **Kathy Mattea**

Do it for yourself, not the audience. Other recordings of note: Guy Clark.

There is a kind of maturity everywhere evident in Country songs, and one surface of this maturity reflects a knowing that death is inevitable. There is also an awareness that death, though not to be wished for or invited, may be willingly attempted. A belief in heaven shapes some of this territory, but not all.

Desperados Waiting for a Train .... Guy Clark

The train is death and it is coming. You might as well try to rob it: get yourself a few friends, sing a few songs, love on a few bodies, and tell a few lies.

Little Black Train .... Freakwater

Death is inevitable and a prelude to judgment. It is coming—the little steam engine that can and always will.

'Til I'm Too Old to Die Young................. Kieran Kane

This is a non-death wish, an elemental plea. Accepting that death will come, this song attempts to negotiate the terms. This song reflects 1980s awareness of too many early losses of life. Written by Kevin Welch and John Hadley.

The White Dove..................... The Stanley Brothers

The narrator promises to live his life in sorrow because his parents have died.

Mother's Only Sleeping .... Bill Monroe

The death of parents brings a kind of freedom as well as bearable loss. Death accepted as a patient wait for Jesus.

The Year that Clayton Delaney Died............ Tom T. Hall

After the death of his mentor, a young man imagines a heaven peopled with drunken guitar pickers. The abiding memory of loss inspires achievement.

Please Don't Bury Me....................... John Prine

Prine stakes his claim to being the first person in heaven to show the angels his ass. Maybe God likes a little raucous laughter, too.

MY COUNTRY ROOTS

Rosewood Casket . . . . **Dolly Parton, Linda Rondstadt, & Emmylou Harris**

Two very different caskets are twinned and entwined in this song: a small box containing love letters and the larger box that will, perhaps soon, contain the woman the letters are written to. The images are macabre but the sentiment is sweet. Loss of life is not true loss—it is only a sleep to awaken in a better place.

Will the Roses Bloom Where She Lies Sleeping. . . . . **Ricky Skaggs & Tony Rice**

A celebration of love that requires two graves to die.

Digging Up Bones . . . .**Randy Travis**

Love dies, yeah, but is love-exhumed a different story altogether? That's a fresh image—an honest marriage between two of Country's dearest themes.

Ballad of Forty Dollars. . . . . **Charlie Sizemore**

All debts do not end at the grave; the dead man owed the gravedigger forty dollars.

Jim, I Wore a Tie Today . . . . **The Highwaymen**

Friends, fellow gold prospectors, together face death and encounter life, until one, inevitably, has to continue on without the other.

Don't Bury Me on the Lone Prairie . . . . **The Carter Family**

Over and over again, the dying make demands on the living.

Bury Me Beneath the Willow. . . . . . **Ricky Skaggs & Tony Rice**

A wish for this earth to be a conclusion.

Flyin' Shoes. . . . . **Lyle Lovett**

Death gives us flying shoes. Question is, do they fly us to peace, or are they just what we vanish in? Townes van Zandt wrote this wonder.

Oh, Death. . . . .**Ralph Stanley and the Clinch Mountain Boys**

Death is no respecter of station. All beg before it when it comes early.

Will the Circle Be Unbroken ...... The Nitty Gritty Dirt Band
(Featuring All Stars)

Death is both a part of the circle of life and a primary cause of pain in life. If God is the great undertaker, and death no respecter of persons, we human beings owe a lot to each other.

MY COUNTRY ROOTS

86 God

In the world of Country, God, quite specifically, means a Protestant Christian God preferably a Baptist, a Methodist, a Presbyterian, or an Episcopalian. While God the Father and his son Jesus make frequent appearances in Country, the Bible itself makes far more.

I Saw the Light . . . . **Hank Williams**

The elemental Country praise song of witness to one's own transformation after an encounter with Jesus. Self-loathing gives way to God-living. Praise the Lord!

Amazing Grace . . . . **Hee Haw Gospel Quartet**

Penned by a slave trader who had an "I Saw the Light" experience, this hymn captures the sheer surprise of a self-loathing wretch encountering God's unearned, undeserved presence as it gives him a loving, human heart.

Dropkick Me Jesus. . . . .**Bobby Bare**

A modern, macho "Amazing Grace." A man wants to be God's football. He imagines the saints as his offensive line—and God's toe, well, that's the grace. This song reflects a powerful sense that human beings are not so much wicked as powerless.

Using My Bible for a Roadmap . . . .**Bad Livers**

A song that couldn't exist before the widespread popularity of automobiles, it simply insists that the Bible applies quite literally to the modern world. Life is a journey to heaven and the Bible is the roadmap.

Take Me in Your Lifeboat. . . . .**The Country Gentlemen**

This vivid maritime image takes a mountain people and a desert people back to the time of Noah. One can imagine this being written on a very rainy afternoon.

Get Up, John . . . . **Emmylou Harris**

Not a song to Jesus, but a song in Jesus's voice. Wild and beautiful, Emmylou Harris impersonates God speaking to John.

John the Revelator. . . . .**Son House**

A song about a man, John, who told a few of God's secrets. Performed here by one of the great blues legends of all time.

Tribulations . . . . Jerry Douglas & Peter Rowan

Fire from heaven, blood filled sea, and Jesus carrying the believer home to heaven.

Get Down on Your Knees and Pray . . . . .Bill Monroe

Simple instruction, but perhaps received with a degree of complexity by a people who have been on their knees to beg.

The Great Speckled Bird . . . . Roy Acuff

Embracing absurd theology, this ode is to the dappled, despised bird who promises that a savior will descend from heaven and she, the odd bird, will transport those who believe to the savior's heaven, singing a song never before heard.

Fish and Whistle. . . . . John Prine

Life is absurd; then we die; then we get to fish in heaven. This song suggests that salvation requires action on man's part and God's part. *You forgive us, we'll forgive you.* Hidden in this hymn of hope for a sweet heaven are old Job-like concerns: why is there war? why is love rare? why do bees sting? why are we afraid? Doubt and faith co-exist in this song.

Mansions for Me. . . . . .Bill Monroe

Earthly envy is assuaged by the assurance that God will provide mansions for all. The choice of the word "hut" to describe home breathes fresh air into the "heavenly mansion" wish.

This World Is Not My Home . . .Jim Lauderdale, Ralph Stanley, & The Clinch Mountain Boys

Death is a homecoming. Jesus is an expectant host for a weak, poor earthling who heeds the beckoning of angels. Heaven is the home that death transports us to.

Mercedes. . . . . Janis Joplin

A passionate plea to God to provide material luxuries. This is a stark critique of God as a road to wealth—in this world or the next.

Working on a Building . . . . .The Seldom Scene

The only thing we know for sure: Neither liars, gamblers, drunkards, nor preachers are *not* doing it. The song seems to say there's something we need to do and something God needs to do if God and man are gonna get together.

MY COUNTRY ROOTS

No Depression . . . . **Uncle Tupelo**

All the traditional clichés: heaven as home, the dark hour, tribulation, judgment near, and yet the whole song is an original, catalyzed by a phrase, "no depression," which has multiple meanings.

God's Coloring Book . . . . **Dolly Parton**

The world is God's toy. A silent God creates visual beauty and lovely colors to announce the presence of his spirit.

Jerusalem Tomorrow . . . .**David Olney**

This extraordinary Jesus song isn't about Jesus at all. It's about a trickster-charlatan in some desert town like Phoenix, or Vegas, who encounters a man with nothing to sell. "Amazing Grace" for the dubious.

In My Hour of Darkness . . . .**Gram Parsons**

This is a cryptic, apocalyptic prayer-poem from the cosmic Country boy. Parsons had both vision and speed. Perhaps he had God. He seems to have had an answered prayer.

What We Sound Like

Don't believe the myth that all Country sounds the same. Nothing could be more inaccurate. Listening to any one of our playlists in its entirety, you will hear echoes of many influences: from the old time music of Appalachia to zydeco from Louisiana; from black gospel and blues music to white gospel and shape-note hymn-singing; from the raw California sound of Bakersville honky tonks to the silky Bob Wills's swing-your-partner sounds of Oklahoma. Country varies. Traditional bluegrass never has a drum; countrypolitan is never without one. Use of a banjo, a steel guitar, or a fiddle may give a song a Country sound, but so can a classical (cello and violin) string section when Owen Bradley is the producer. Insiders joke that the best definition of a Country song is "three chords and the truth." Three chords can be played and produced a lot of different ways. Holding all these country variations together is an understanding on the part of Country musicians and Country audiences that there is an authenticity, a raw truth, a hard beauty that can be played and communicated as Country. Country music has an evolving sound. It is ever negotiating and renegotiating the terms of its relationship with mainstream and marginal musical forms. From its oft-overlooked origins, to its contemporary idiosyncrasies, the following lists survey some of the most important eras and disparate subgenres that have contributed to the Country canon. What do we sound like? We sound different. We sound different from each other, and from you—if you're not Country.

87 Country Blues

The Outsider Element

Both Bill Monroe and Hank Williams were strongly influenced by local blues musicians and guitar players in their hometowns. Country owes much of its twang and mournful, moaning sound to the blues. Blues lent Country music the requisite confidence needed to admit to being an outsider—socially, economically, and culturally. Most importantly, blues is an expression of pain and desire for liberation.

Going to Move to Alabama . . . . Charley Patton

In its purest form, Country is the blues. One need only to listen to the recordings of Mississippi's Charley Patton to hear where Hank Williams found inspiration. Compare this to "Move It on Over," and the influence is clear.

In the Pines. . . . . Leadbelly

Bill Monroe made this Leadbelly tune a Country and bluegrass standard—just one example of the shared subject matter, styles, and songbooks of the two genres.

WHAT WE SOUND LIKE

Travellin' Blues. . . . .**Jimmie Rodgers**

How do you get Country? Take a blues song and add a fiddle and a yodel in the middle. No one bridged the blues and Country like Rodgers, "The Singing Brakeman"—one of Country's earliest trailblazers.

Sitting on Top of the World. . . . . **Roscoe Holcombe**

Here, a father of American folk music employs the favored instrument of the earliest blues musicians—the banjo. A bluegrass anthem on the theme of perseverance.

You Can't Get Stuff No More. . . . . **Blind Willie McTell**

A master of Country Blues swing, McTell's high tenor and chorus harmonies exemplify the implied bridge between Delta blues and western swing.

Blue Yodel #1 (T for Texas). . . . .**Jimmie Rodgers**

This straight-up blues lyric drives a gothic lament about a cheating woman. He's gone mad, and he's going for his gun.

Worried Man Blues. . . . . **The Carter Family**

The first family of Country reminds us that if you haven't lived it, you can't sing it—perhaps it's the hard-rural living that most unifies the cultures of Country and the blues.

Lovesick Blues. . . . . **Hank Williams**

Hank's signature tune takes the straight meditative form of Country Blues, and winds it into a multi-part verse, chorus bridge form. In other words, he adds a little "pop" to the Blues and winds up with Country.

Johnny B. Goode. . . . . **Chuck Berry**

The backwoods guitar prodigy in this Chuck Berry classic unearths Country and blues' shared narrative of the homegrown, soulful instrumentalist who creates success and fame out of artistic prowess.

Po' Lazarus. . . . . **Bright Light Quartet**

At their roots, blues and country songs provide secular outlets of expression—alternatives to gospel music. Here are both a black gospel and a white gospel version of the same song. Both traditions had their influence on country.

Wabash Cannonball . . . . Roy Acuff

Whereas the slide guitar—originally a piece of fence wire strung between two nails on the side of a barn—provided the lonesome moan for the Blues, the dobro created the same effect for Country. This Acuff tune was his most-well known.

Mining Camp Blues. . . . . Hazel Dickens and Alice Gerrard

Whether hunched over, picking cotton in a hot Mississippi field, or ducked down, blasting coal in a West Virginia mine, both the blues and Country draw much of their lyrical inspiration from the struggles of hard-time labor.

Milk Cow Blues. . . . . Bob Wills

Another song that Country adapted from the blues, this tune uses the harsh metaphor of a barnyard cow for a woman. This one is a call-and-response version from the King of Texas Swing—but be sure to hear Fred McDowell's version, and Roscoe Holcombe's too.

Country Blues . . . . Doc Watson

On this straight-up blues tune, Watson shows his ability to drop a thumb, with his claw hammer-style banjo playing a la Dock Boggs.

House of the Rising Sun. . . . . Ramblin' Jack Elliott

A Country blues tune about a house of ill-repute in New Orleans, this song is also known as "The Rising Sun Blues."

Far Away Eyes. . . . . The Rolling Stones

The Stones paint us a Country blues caricature of love and redemption, revealing that their early explorations of Robert Johnson were inseparable from their explorations of Hank Williams.

Midnight Rider . . . . The Allman Brothers

Whether a convict, a hobo, or a traveler on the Underground Railroad, the notion of a fleeing "midnight rider" suits both Country and blues—this from a band that epitomizes the crossroads between the two genres.

Long Gone Lonesome Blues. . . . . Hank Williams, Jr.

The son sings the father's song, reminding us all that Country is the blues.

88 | Old Time

The British Isles Meet the Appalachian Mountains

Old time is the traditional mountain music of Appalachia. based on the canon of British Isles ballads and fiddle tunes brought across the Atlantic Ocean. This is the sound of generational communities—it is the tie that binds. One part instrumental, one part lyrical narrative, old time lacks the aggressive individualism of bluegrass, and is a rougher, less symmetrical, and more meditative form of Country.

Johnson Boys . . . . **The Freight Hoppers**

An upbeat fiddle tune one might hear at a square dance or a fiddle contest—staples of old time—featuring the hot-picking of this North Carolina string-band. Now, a fiddler who can "buck dance" while he's sawing on the strings—that's tough to beat.

Go On, Nora Lee . . . . **Uncle Dave Macon**

The Grand Ole Opry's first big star, Macon was largely responsible for bringing the primitive roots of Country to a popular audience. This is a song that echoes the fiddle tunes of Appalachia.

Fall on My Knees . . . . **Fred Cockerman, Oscar Jenkins, & Tommy Jarrell**

A standard from the old time songbook about love, this traditional lays vivid blues verse over a cyclical fiddle tune—a trademark of old time.

The Blackest Crow . . . . **Tim O'Brien**

A haunting ballad from the British Isles, this haunting love letter of devotion not only reveals Country's lyrical and poetic strength, but also its melodic range. A gorgeous song with a profound and timeless resonance.

Shootin' Creek . . . . **Charlie Poole**

The same tune as "Cripple Creek," an old time standard, this "copy-cat" exemplifies the existence of a vital oral tradition. Songs migrated from country to country and mountain to mountain. The details or titles might change, but the melody and fiddle part remain pretty much the same.

Poor Ellen Smith . . . . **Hobart Smith**

A documentation of a late nineteenth century Appalachian murder, this ballad has become a standard of old time and bluegrass musicians alike. Much like stained-glass windows in the medieval age, the songs of Appalachia often served as the newspaper headlines and histories for Mountain folk.

Boll Weevil . . . . Fred Cockerman, Oscar Jenkins, & Tommy Jarrell

Cursing the natural obstacles faced in agricultural labor, this song indicts a pest that's the subject of many old time and blues songs.

Wildwood Flower . . . . Mother Maybelle Carter

The auto-harp was a favored and easy-to-learn instrument that could accompany any traditional mountain ballad. No song exemplifies the instrument more than this Mother Maybelle tune. A major Country composition.

Angel Band . . . . .The Stanley Brothers

Often categorized as bluegrass, the Stanleys' roots were nourished by the old time music that circulated through the southeast Virginia mountains they called home. Here a song that reflects old time's gospel sounds, as well as stirring, almost-Native American harmonies—no doubt influenced by the primitive shaped-note singing in white rural churches.

Going Up on the Mountain. . . . . Jody Stecher

For many a mountain man, it's the peak that represents redemption and salvation—feel-good liberation theology for the solitary woman or man. If you don't know Stecher's music, you should.

The Green Rolling Hills of West Virginia . . . . . .Hazel Dickens & Alice Gerrard

Conjuring the sounds of an old mountain home with silvery autoharp and dynamic, sister-like harmonies, Hazel Dickens and Alice Gerard represent the Appalachian sound with a powerful authenticity.

Billy Gray. . . . . .Norman Blake

A master of old time Appalachian music, Blake's uncanny ability to write lyrics in the mode of original traditional ballads is unrivaled. He's a helluva good guitar picker, too. Here, a story song that could have come over on the Mayflower.

MY COUNTRY ROOTS

Wish We Had Our Time Again ....John Hartford

A guardian and innovator of the Appalachian songbook, Hartford loved writing fiddle tunes with quirky, amusing lyrics in the mold of "Cotton Eyed Joe." Nostalgia is a familiar theme in mountain music.

Miner's Refrain...........................Gillian Welch

A true student of Country's many sub-genres, Welch uses a simple guitar and two-part, lonesome harmony to focus an Appalachian hardship: coal mines.

Little Black Train ....Freakwater

This contemporary group is often categorized as alternative Country but on this Carter Family classic, they display their traditional old time mountain roots.

John Henry...............................The Mammals

These contemporary old timers update the form by adding drums and electric bass to songs from the traditional songbook, delivering hard-driving renditions of old time standards.

89 Bluegrass

The Train: Integral Parts Working Together

This particular style of Country music combines British Isles fiddle music, Country blues, appalachian old time, and what's often referred to as the "high lonesome" sound—most noted in the characteristic tenor stylings of Bill Monroe. Often inappropriately referred to as "hillbilly" music, bluegrass is fueled by a rugged sense of individualism and pride that can be heard in the hard-driving rhythms, tight two-part harmonies, and break-out solos on the fiddle, mandolin, and banjo—solos rarely heard in old time music. Loud, and often brash, bluegrass comes self-amplified.

Blue Moon of Kentucky . . . . Bill Monroe

The original bluegrass super-hit, made most famous by Elvis, but offered here by its inventor, "The Father of Bluegrass," Monroe uses his haunting tenor to reach the moon and conjure its curse.

How Mountain Girls Can Love . . . . The Stanley Brothers

If pride is a centerpiece of the bluegrass psyche, there's nothing more important to mountain men than their women. The Stanleys' heavily accented harmonies shout a message that might carry from mountain top to mountain top.

Roll in My Sweet Baby's Arms . . . . Flatt & Scruggs

This young man's trading in his shovel and hoe for the day-dreaming fantasy of a lover. The anticipation of the mail train and the promise it brings offers hope and salvation. Scruggs revolutionized the banjo with his melodic, three-finger picking that transformed a rhythm instrument into a lead soloist. Listen to it roll.

Satan's Jeweled Crown . . . . The Louvin Brothers

Though considered progressive, bluegrass has never forgotten its religious roots, and the Louvins always remained firmly grounded in the darker biblical tales. Perhaps their harmonies are the most unique and haunting of all the brother acts.

You Don't Know My Mind . . . . Jimmy Martin

The story of Jimmy Martin is a complex one. Although now deceased, Martin is still considered one of the greatest high-tenors in bluegrass of all time, although he was a loner and a pariah in the establishment's eyes. His style of bluegrass was hard-driving and his voice could saw timber, as evidenced in this great song.

WHAT WE SOUND LIKE

Roll Muddy River .... Osborne Brothers

Brother acts are an essential component of the bluegrass tradition—namely for the natural ability of blood relatives to sing close-knit, high-lonesome harmonies. The Osbornes do so as well as any in this tune that features their fine banjo and mandolin picking.

White Dove .... Old and in the Way

If there were a bluegrass hymnal, this song would be on the very first page. Written by Carter Stanley, it's performed here by the super-group that helped attract counter-culture hippies to traditional mountain music.

Doing My Time .... The Seldom Scene

A meditative, earnest blues devoted to the Sisyphean struggles of life on a chain gang. This song proves that few bands in the history of bluegrass music mastered the art of vocal harmony as well as these Virginia boys—I dare you to try and hold a note longer.

More Pretty Girls Than One...... Ricky Skaggs and Tony Rice

A must-own song from a must-own album entitled *Skaggs and Rice*. Bluegrass lyrics use an upbeat positivity that old time usually won't. Representative of the genre's big city appeal, certainly this these lyrics might prove true in town more than in the country.

Old Train .... The Tony Rice Unit

Composed of the greatest pickers and players around, Tony Rice's third-generation all-star group reinterpreted the genre with a technical flair and proficiency unrivaled in its history. Simply put, the best picking in bluegrass music on a classic song about bluegrass's biggest fascination: the train.

Way Downtown .... Doc Watson

Watson, along with the late Clarence White, brought fast, complicated fiddle melodies to the guitar, effectively turning a rhythm instrument into a soloist. A staple of bluegrass music since, the flat-pick guitar never sounded better than off of Doc's old Gallagher.

Pick Me Up on Your Way Down .... Del McCoury

Bluegrass pickers have adopted this Harlan Howard song as their own, no doubt because of its "return-to-your-roots" message. When you hear Del's sweet-soaring tenor, you'll hear a lot of Monroe, no doubt because Del sang side by side with him in the sixties.

Blue Ridge Cabin Home . . . . **Bobby Hicks, J.D. Crowe, Jerry Douglas, etc.**

Nothing represents the old home place like lyric—a self-referential nod to the geographical roots of bluegrass music.

No Hiding Place . . . . **The Nashville Bluegrass Band**

This band displays Bluegrass's inexorable ties to gospel music—add the mandolin, fiddle, and banjo, and an up-tempo beat to your favorite hymns and you've got a feel-good gospel message. A must-listen that might have you jumping in the river.

Every Time You Say Goodbye. . . . . **Alison Krauss**

Easily Bluegrass's biggest contemporary star, and one of Country's most respected and consistently successful artists, Krauss began as a child-prodigy bluegrass fiddler and has never forgotten her mountain roots, even if she's smoothed them out a bit.

Landslide. . . . . **Dixie Chicks**

This tough-Texas threesome has proven time and again that acoustic music and bluegrass instrumentation can be both commercially and artistically viable—they prove here how adaptable classic pop songs are to the bluegrass format, re-imagining this timeless Fleetwood Mac hit.

WHAT WE SOUND LIKE

90 Honky Tonk

Country's Original Bar Music

Though the origins of the word are debatable, a honky tonk has always been a bar that features live music of some sort. Whether "tonks" were Black American establishments, and "honky" was added to segregate, or whether the name came from the brand name Tonk piano, manufactured by Ernest Tonk at the turn of the century, Honky tonk incorporates blues stylings, Country instruments, and a heavy accented down-beat, preferable for dancing. The subject matter usually has to do with drinking, partying, cheating or crying, and almost always features "Hawaiian" steel guitar.

Honky Tonk Blues . . . . **Jelly Roll Morton**

Before it became Country, the term honky-tonk referred to the sound of beat-up bars and pianos, which were often more suited to the driving rhythmic stylings of rag-time jazz. In this song, one of the genre's greatest composers reveals Country's roots in early jazz and blues on the foundational instrument of honky tonk: the piano.

Honky Tonk Blues . . . . **Hank Williams**

With the hard-drinking, good-timing, late-night life comes the tough realization of morning—and mourning the loneliness and heartache that ensues. The piano's gone, but if you close your eyes you can hear its strong heavy down-beat in the rhythm section—Hank always knew you gotta give 'em something to dance to.

Honky Tonkin' . . . . **Hank Williams**

The ultimate honky tonk song, by the ultimate honky tonker. This, one of Hank's masterpieces, is a sweet but risky invitation to a sinful night out on the town. The emblematic steel guitar says it all, conjuring up a hard-drinking, smoke-filled retreat for those looking to chase away the blues.

Tennessee Waltz . . . . **Roy Acuff**

One of Country's most-loved melodies and earliest super-hits could be an episode from "Tales From the Honky-tonk." Hawaii's contribution to honky tonk is featured here in the blue, silvery tones of the dobro.

Back Street Affair . . . . **Webb Pierce**

There's no better place than a back-street bar for two lovers to go—and there's no better song to epitomize what Country infidelity sounds like. Pierce's earnest vocals float over the requisite snappy, back-beat rhythms of the acoustic guitar—honky tonk's metronome.

Just Can't Live That Fast Anymore . . . . **Lefty Frizzell**

Here, one of honky tonk's most loyal practitioners gives up on the lifestyle, but won't let go of that trademark slap-bass and steel sound— there's an edgy hop-funk feel to this tune that foreshadows rockabilly.

Honky Tonk Song . . . . **Webb Pierce**

With no money, no love, and nowhere else to go, the door to this broke-down bar is pretty inviting. Simply put, the band won't stop playing, and the piano rolls over a straight-up blues structure that's characteristic of honky tonk.

Mr. Jukebox . . . . **Ernest Tubb**

Some people may say it's just a machine, but when you're all alone with no one else to talk to, that old Wurlitzer in the corner can be a drinking man's best friend. A bittersweet reminder of how automated recordings replaced the live house band at the honky tonk, sung with Tubb's beer-soaked baritone.

Why Baby Why . . . . **George Jones**

In a bit of a role-reversal, it's the woman who's run out on the man and left him home alone to pay the bills—one of honky tonk's greatest songs and most idiosyncratic lyrics, by one of Country's greatest singers. Sometimes honky tonk's got a little hip-hop.

I'm a Honky Tonk Girl . . . . **Loretta Lynn**

Loretta proves that she can honky tonk as well as any man with this stand-up declaration of Country pride. The fiddle, steel, and her sassy drawl tell us so.

Honky Tonk Heroes . . . . **Waylon Jennings**

Here, Waylon yearns for the hard-partying days of his youth, wondering how time slipped away so quickly. Part of a 1970s honky tonk resurgence deemed "outlaw," Waylon was responsible for reclaiming Hank when Country's commercial movement of the 1960s had all but abandoned its roots. A down and dirty sound that marries a bit of rock n' roll funk with his honky tonk roots.

Honky Tonk Man . . . . **Dwight Yoakam**

Dwight reminds us all where his musical roots lay, in this version of a Johnny Horton classic. He loves to dance, drink, and party all night,

MY COUNTRY ROOTS

but without a loyal, forgiving "mama" to come home to, this honk tonk man's got nothing.

Bar Exam . . . . The Derailers

Austin's favorite honky tonkers simultaneously pay tribute to the bar-life and mock the professional, elitist culture alien to them. Their honky tonk sound puts us in the middle of the crowded dance floor.

Dim Lights, Thick Smoke. Jack Ingram

One of honky tonk's contemporary stars sings one of its classic songs—the bar band sounds bigger, and more electric, but the sentiment and soul remains. You get the feeling that Lefty and Hank would approve.

No Train to Memphis BR549

These contemporary honky tonkers put the boot-kicking, hard-driving attitude back into Country, at a time when when the industry seems to have traded in all of its dirty roots for the promise of big pop money—ever a familiar theme in Country. There may not be a train to Memphis anymore, but they sure make it sound like they're rolling down the tracks.

Honky Tonk Girls. . . . . Hank Williams III

Picking up where his grandfather left off, Hank III shows he has more in common with the straight-up honky tonk sound of the 1950s than he does with the Country sound of today. A full-circle return to his roots on this tribute to the company of the hard-partying ladies he and his grandfather kept.

91 Western Swing

When Jazz and Country Had a Baby

Influenced by the popular big band and swing of the 1920s and 1930s, western swing combined the sounds of New Orleans rag-time and jazz with western styled fiddle tunes—all at the service of orchestrating a great dance. Listen for the twin-fiddles, steel guitar, and horns, trademarks of the western swing sound. Oh, and also listen for Bob Wills's immortal "aaa-haa," which is essentially a falsetto "yee-haw." This is a music to glide around a floor to. The Texas two-step, like western swing, is smooth and refined.

Any Old Time . . . . **Jimmie Rodgers**

In this sweet-swinging country blues song, Rodgers shows us what New Orleans shares with Tulsa, namely that Tin Pan Alley melody and big city swing.

Take Me Back to Tulsa . . . . **Bob Wills**

Truly the Father of western swing, Wills, a master fiddler, bandleader, and songwriter, epitomized the genre's unique combination of Dixie jazz, big band, Mexican, and fiddle music into feel-good dance hall tunes. This, his signature song, marks the epicenter of the genre's movement in the 1930s and 1940s.

Faded Love . . . . **Bob Wills**

It's impossible not to include more than one Wills tune, and really there are few love songs as memorable as this anthem, featuring his trademark lead fiddle and the Playboys' heart-wrenching harmonies. A classic.

Shame on You . . . . **Spade Cooley**

Though he never acquired the long-term success of Wills, Cooley rivaled him at one point in the 1940s—starring in several Hollywood movies, and even proclaiming himself the "King Of Swing." His career ended tragically when he was convicted of brutally murdering his wife. Ironically enough, this is the song he was famous for.

Take These Shackles from My Heart . . . . **Pee Wee King**

King, an accomplished polka musician at an early age, easily made the transition to western swing, and is attributed with helping to bring polkas and cowboy songs to mainstream Country. Here he sings about a topic central to the genre: freedom.

Bob Wills Is Still the King . . . . .Asleep At The Wheel

There really is no question who's sits atop the throne of western swing, but this Austin-based band isn't too far from the top—here, a tribute to the influence and sound of the King.

Slippin' Around . . . . Floyd Tillman

A winding swell of melancholy and regret, this song laments the suffering inherent in a cagey love affair, where a man is caught between his wife and the woman he loves. It features the standard, oh-so-lonesome steel-guitar and fiddle harmonies.

When You're Lovin', You're Livin' . . . . Hank Thompson

A bit of country advice in this upbeat, feel-good tune from Thompson shows that a western swing dance tune can be as whimsical lyrically as it is musically. Form swinging function.

Oklahoma Sweetheart Sally Ann . . . . The Maddox Brothers and Rose

A tribute to a sweet Oklahoma maiden, this song showcases the state that served as the center of a musical movement. A fun live rendition here from Rose Maddox, replete with improvisational clapping, and the falsetto "aaa-haaa" Bob Wills made famous.

Stay All Night . . . . Willie Nelson

Who wouldn't want to when the music feels this good? Nelson pays tribute to Wills in this ode to dancing 'til the sun comes up. The playful meter and language of the verse has a hip-hop feel.

That's Right You're Not from Texas . . . . Lyle Lovett

Texas has always had to share its western swing claim with Oklahoma, and as Lyle makes clear in this tune, Texas has a lot of pride but a lot of hospitality, too.

Money Tree . . . . Big Sandy and His Flyrite Boys

A hip, swinging tune about the wild hopes of a poor man looking to pick his money off a backyard branch. This fantastic band sounds like a cross between Blind Willie McTell and Bob Wills.

Down the Trail of San Antone . . . . Riders in the Sky

Contemporary masters of all things cowboy and western, this trio blends their high harmonies and sweet double fiddles on this western swing classic, proving that the sound is alive and well today.

92 Nashville Sound

The Death of Honky Tonk

Nashville sound is the 1950s sound that abandoned much of everything "hillbilly" in Country in an attempt to create broad commercial, popular appeal. It has much the same relationship to Country as Motown does to blues and rhythm and blues. The style attributed to producers Chet Atkins and Owen Bradley was simple: no banjos, mandolins, or fiddles, and nothing twangy. Bass, guitar, drums, piano, big reverb-heavy vocals, harmonies, and the occasional orchestral flourish were the trademark sounds. The movement also employed professional session musicians into recording sessions—players who brought sophisticated, smooth chops and a willingness to work for the producer. Suddenly, Country sounded less provincial and more pop, just as country folk a decade beyond the big war and out of the Depression took their places in cities and offices and factories in a larger, more modern world.

Oh Lonesome Me . . . . Don Gibson

Loneliness doesn't feel so bad on this upbeat, carefree Gibson hit, delivered with a hint of sarcasm, irony, and a load of those poppy harmonies that gave Country its big crossover commercial appeal.

I Fall to Pieces . . . . Patsy Cline

Easily one of Country's most beautiful songs, this Owen Bradley-produced tune about the psychological torture of heartbreak is a text book lesson in the Nashville sound—a jazz rhythm combo, a smoothed-out, twang-less steel guitar, and big harmonies. Cline was the first superstar of the new sound.

King of the Road . . . . Roger Miller

No one toed the line between Country and pop better than Miller, and this, his most successful and immortal song, combines Country subject matter—the life of train-hopping rambler—with a stripped down, spacious pop arrangement and production style.

It Wasn't God Who Made Honky Tonk Angels . . . . . Kitty Wells

A honky tonk song never sounded so sophisticated and classy as in this Kitty Wells classic about the negative influence of bad men on good women. Classic Nashville sound formula—Country lyric, Country vocal, pop arrangement and instrumentation, no banjo, no steel.

Walk On By . . . . **Leroy Van Dyke**

One of the most successful Country singles of all time, sung by a professional auctioneer-turned-Country-star, this tune presents the psychological pains of having to sneak around and cheat for your love.

What's He Doing in My World . . . . **Eddy Arnold**

The character in this story is either playing dumb, or he's just plain dumb. Another man's moving in on his woman—stealing kisses in front of him—and still, the refrain. Classic Nashville sound vocal.

He'll Have to Go . . . .**Jim Reeves**

Reeves's warm baritone never sounded smoother than on this Country classic—yet another tale of a man moving in on another's woman, all delivered with the confidence and courage the fella in the previous song could have used.

For the Good Times . . . . **Ray Price**

Classic super-smooth, yet bold, Nashville sound on the Kris Kristofferson masterpiece that Price, among many others, made into a hit. Facing the inevitable, a man pleads with his lover to share a final intimate moment together before the hard reality of separation sinks in.

I'm Sorry . . . . **Brenda Lee**

A teenage girl never sounded so convincing and heartbroken as on this number one crossover hit of regret. Almost all traces of the traditional Country sound have been stripped away.

Still. . . . . **Bill Anderson**

It's no wonder how "Whispering Bill" got his nickname—his trademark-spoken, err, whispered lyric lends a testimonial conviction to a statement of devotion. A good example of how pop production styles obscured Country's roots—you might be asking, "Is this Country?"

Seven Spanish Angels . . . . **Ray Charles & Willie Nelson**

The spirit of the Nashville sound revisited in this stirring and sweeping duet, decades after the sound's inception. Perhaps Ray Charles's *Modern Sounds in Country and Western* best represents that crossover pop sound as it matured past its zenith, leaving a lush afterglow.

93 Countrypolitan

More Pop!

Country has always been conflicted about its roots perhaps concerned that the twang and "hillbilly" elements narrow its profit margins, perhaps concerned that pronounced regionalism limits some listeners' ability to "get" the song if it sounds too foreign. Countrypolitan is really just an extension of the Nashville sound, but with an even greater stress put on pop song structures, spearheaded by famed producers Billy Sherrill and Glen Sutton. One of Country's most fertile and controversial periods, it also happens to feature some of its greatest stars from the 1960s, 1970s, and early 1980s.

Til I Get it Right . . . . Tammy Wynette

Lush strings, graceful flamenco guitar, and group harmonies create the foundation for this, a classic countrypolitan song.

Does My Ring Hurt Your Finger . . . . Charley Pride

One of the defining characteristics of any subgenre of Country is the way diction is used. Are accents banished or exaggerated? Here, the classic country drawl is gone, and the words are sung straight in an appeal to a wider audience.

A White Sport Coat . . . . Marty Robbins

A classic countrypolitan song utilizes the lush backup singers, enormous amounts of reverb on the vocals, and leaves almost all of its Country roots at the recording studio door.

Lost Her Love on Our First Date . . . . Conway Twitty

Twitty explored a lot of musical styles to accommodate his songwriting, as is the case here in what feels like a slow dance number at a sock hop. This song reveals his roots as a rock 'n' roll teen idol, but that reminds us that Elvis considered himself to be a Country singer.

Commercial Affection . . . . Mel Tillis

With a heavy dose of unintended irony, this countrypolitan single simultaneously sheds light on the movement's purpose and its limitations.

Big Girls Don't Cry . . . . Lynn Anderson

Candy-coated, call-and-response vocals on this falsetto, calliope-like chorus from an oft-overlooked but important contributor to the countrypolitan sound. You get the feeling that Anderson, whose strong

Southern accent is apparent in many of her songs, hid her natural Country drawl to give this song more pop appeal.

Where I Ought to Be . . . . .Skeeter Davis

In this track, virtually all of the elements of earlier Country music have been taken away except the song structure itself.

Make the World Go Away. Eddy Arnold

Some considered Arnold to have the best voice in Country music even though his arrangements, vocal delivery, and song choices were very neutral. An interesting tidbit: Arnold was managed by Col. Tom Parker, who also managed Elvis.

Sea of Heartbreak. . . . . .Don Gibson

Gibson is best known for penning this song and the Patsy Cline hit "Sweet Dreams." Check out Tom Petty's version and Johnny Cash's, too—a contrast clearly reveals much about the countrypolitan style.

Don't It Make My Brown Eyes Blue. . . . . Crystal Gayle

This song, a hit for Loretta Lynn's younger, more sophisticated-appearing sister, is essentially a jazz song structure wrapped up in a Country-pop production. One of countrypolitan's goals was to take Country artists and to earn them larger audiences on the pop charts. This song is a perfect example. Less Country, more cosmopolitan = huge hit.

Daytime Friends . . . . .Kenny Rogers

A good example of countrypolitan's ability to adapt production styles to individual artists and still keep it more pop than Country, this song has lots of guitars, big vocals, and a smoothed-out delivery. Sonically and stylistically, Rogers's number one hit has more in common with The Eagles than with Hank, but then again the Eagles are a Country rock band.

Love Is Like a Butterfly . . . . Dolly Parton

Parton's career began at the end of the countrypolitan movement. In this song, counterpoint group harmonies, a cascading piano line, and psychedelic lyrics lead the listener to believe that this song might have been recorded in San Francisco, not Nashville. This is Country spreading its wings and its appeal to a wide audience.

94 | Rockabilly

Honky tonk's younger punk cousin, rockabilly is a unique blend of hillbilly Country and early rock n' roll. In fact, many believe it to be the original precursor of Rock 'n' Roll. It is nervous, frenzied; it can be angry, celebratory or both; but mostly it's just plain wiggly. In its current form, it is as much a retro lifestyle and fashion statement as it is a style of Country.

Hound Dog . . . . .Elvis Presley

The "King of Rock 'n' Roll" became the king because he found a way to amplify blues music with the sounds of Country. If you listen closely, this song is rockabilly, what with the walking bass and the guitar leads, but soon after it was recorded people started calling it rock 'n' roll. An earlier version of note is by Big Mama Thornton.

Train of Love . . . . .Johnny Cash

Like many who recorded their first records at Sun Studios in Memphis, Tennessee, Cash's early sound was decidedly rockabilly. Eventually, as his music matured, he fused the sounds of rockabilly with the mountain ballads and gospels of his youth to create his legendary sound.

Blue Suede Shoes . . . . Carl Perkins

One of the defining characteristics of rockabilly is its screaming electric guitar. Perkins's guitar playing certainly influenced the style. Before rockabilly became popular, the electric guitar took solos in Country arrangements, but never with such audacity, aggression and strength.

Whole Lot of Shakin' Going On . . . . Jerry Lee Lewis

Nicknamed "The Killer," Lewis could play a piano through a concrete wall. He rebelled against his fundamental Christian upbringing and brought out his aggression through energetic, bullet-paced playing and singing that drove the shrieking girls crazy.

Sam's Place . . . . Buck Owens

Owens was responsible for creating his own style of Country, "The Bakersfield Sound," out of equal parts rockabilly and countrypolitan. He took the single guitar of rockabilly music and doubled it with twin telecaster guitars, a distinct sound that continues to define his California Country style.

WHAT WE SOUND LIKE

Honky Tonk Man . . . . **Johnny Horton**

Like Jimmie Rogers, Horton was well before his time, playing a style of music that didn't yet have its own name. What others called honky tonk was really rockabilly before rockabilly had a name.

No Train to Memphis **BR549**

This Nashville band got their name from the truck license plate in the opening credits of *Hee Haw*. Fast driving steel guitar, warm harmonies, and air-tight arrangements make this one of the premier rockabilly bands around today.

Broke Down South of Dallas . . . . **Junior Brown**

Brown invented a double-necked half-guitar/half-steel guitar to accommodate his ferocious style of hot rockabilly guitar picking. A contemporary master of the genre.

I'd Rather Die Young . . . . **Jason and the Scorchers**

Nashville's first and most reputable punk band really isn't rockabilly in the truest sense except for the fact that their music is filled with the same defiance and attitude that made the subgenre possible—which in some small way probably made Jason and the Scorchers possible.

T. Rex Boogie . . . . **Rosie Flores**

Rockabilly with a Latin twist. Flores's voice, hot guitar leads, and flirty charm will grab you and shake you around the room.

Big City Good Timin' Gal . . . . **Wayne Hancock**

Even though Hancock and others will tell you that they play country music the way it should be played, he lands on this list because of his unmistakably rockabilly beats. He is one of the best of the few still playing in this style.

7 Months, 39 Days . . . . **Hank Williams III**

The third generation descendent combines his grandfather's voice and soul with this father's attitude in what is truly compelling music—let's call it head-banging honky tonk. Catch a show and you just might get one set of honky tonk or rockabilly and another that's hardcore punk. A must-listen.

Go Hog Wild . . . . **The Legendary Shack Shakers**

Perhaps these young torch bearers best-represent rockabilly's staying power. Certainly, the style and title of this song sums up what rockabilly's all about: one part Hank Williams, one-part Chuck Berry, and one part Sid Vicious.

95 Outlaw

A Strong Reaction to Country Pop

Outlaws are those artists who fought the Country corporate center throughout their careers. A loosely-defined movement, primarily led by Willie Nelson and Waylon Jennings, this genre is rooted in honest song-writing, a no-nonsense attitude, and an unabashed commitment to difference. Here, you'll find some of the artists whose rugged individualism and artistry fueled their tireless pursuit of authentic sounds and songs, whatever the cost. This also happens to be a master-list of country songwriting.

Mind Your Own Business . . . . Hank Williams

Hank infused his songs with a feisty attitude that's clear in this song—back off and keep your opinions to yourself. He's gonna do what he wants, and it's no concern of yours—an outlaw's mantra, through and through.

Cocaine Blues . . . . Johnny Cash

Some say Cash is the original outlaw of Country music. His deep voice, dark garments, and general disrespect for bureaucratic authority, along with songs like this one, changed country music in a good, "bad" way, forever.

Rated X . . . . Loretta Lynn

The "Queen of the Outlaws" knew no boundaries when it came to expressing her mind. In a time when the Country female artist's role was to convey femininity and domesticity, she took on such subjects as abortion, teenage virginity, and divorce, as is the case with this song. She holds the honor of having more songs banned by country music than any other musician. Loretta recently reaffirmed her outlaw royalty by making a critically-acclaimed rock record with Jack White of the White Stripes.

The Silver Tongued Devil and I . . . . Kris Kristofferson

Kristofferson is a profound wordsmith, and definitely the only outlaw who attended Oxford University on a Rhodes scholarship. This beautiful barroom ballad reads like a sixteenth century poem set in a dingy old Nashville bar.

Are You Sure Hank Done It This Way . . . . . . Waylon Jennings

Here, one of the founders of the outlaw movement questions the "Country-ness" of those Nashville sound, pop productions.

The Black Rose (The Devil Made Me Do It) . . . . Billy Joe Shaver

Billy Joe Shaver is probably the most important outlaw you never heard of, at least from a songwriting standpoint. Waylon Jennings brought his music to the mainstream when he recorded a whole album of his songs on *Honky-Tonk Heroes*. This is one of his finest,

Outlaw Women . . . . Hank Williams, Jr.

Part of the charm and allure of outlaw music is that, tonally, it dwells in the shadows and darker spaces of the soul.

Copperhead Road . . . . Steve Earle

With notable exceptions, outlaw music faded away in the 80s. Nonetheless, Earle, who recorded this song about marijuana farming with tools learned in Vietnam, meets all the criteria for outlaw status.

Hands on the Wheel . . . . Willie Nelson

The outlaw's prayer, this song about life and love is lonesome, candid, self-reflective, and at peace with the oh-so-fickle and wild world we live in. A true masterpiece.

Are the Good Times Really Over . . . . Merle Haggard

One of the predominant themes of this song and this music is the lost golden years of American culture. Merle spares no punches when it comes to speaking the truth about good love, good bars, quality work, and respect for the common man.

Tennessee Whiskey . . . . David Allan Coe

You can't get more whiskey-bent and hell-bound than David Allan Coe. Known to ride a motorcycle into the clubs where he was performing in a rhinestone suit and a batman mask, here Coe is more brooding and pensive, giving thanks to the woman he loves and the liquor he drinks.

Lonesome On'ry and Mean . . . . Steve Young

One of the lesser known outlaws, Young was more influential as a songwriter than a performer. Waylon Jennings made this outlaw anthem legendary.

Storms Never Last. . . . . Waylon Jennings & Jessi Colter

Waylon and Jessi were the first couple of outlaw music. The combination of her high-pitched lilting voice with Waylon's velvet and brooding baritone is unlike any duo sound in all of Country music—soulful, graceful, and fragile meets wild and original.

WHAT WE SOUND LIKE

11 Months and 29 Days . . . .**Johnny Paycheck**

Early in life, Paycheck served time in an Ohio prison for shooting a man. This song about a man getting ready to serve his sentence features a wailing harp, which is a signature of the outlaw sound.

96 Country Rock

Country Meets the Counter Culture

During the late 1960s and early 1970s, some Country-influenced artists felt they had more in common with the brash honesty of rock music than they did with the countrypolitan sound that dominated Nashville. Unified by shared musical and political/cultural persuasions, these artists represent the music responsible for marrying the sounds of Hank Williams and Bill Monroe to late 60s and 70s hippie culture.

Return of the Grievous Angel . . . . Gram Parsons

Parsons called his sound "cosmic American." Musically speaking, it was Country to the core, but stylistically and aesthetically he was a rock 'n' roller—a cult figure, and a pioneer of Country rock, especially as a frontman of the Byrds.

Dire Wolf . . . . The Grateful Dead

This Bay Area psychedelic band—often associated with hippies and LSD—actually began as an old time jug-band. They never forgot their Country roots as proven in this great story song about a deadly card game with a wolf.

Ain't No More Cane . . . . Bob Dylan and The Band

This song would fit well on our Lost South / Return South list and demonstrates how the Band and Bob Dylan collaborated to merge their rock aesthetic with raw Country roots.

Take It Easy . . . . The Eagles

The Eagles' fusion of lush country harmonies and easy-flowing acoustic rock arrangements made them one of the most popular bands of the late 1970s and early 1980s.

Two More Bottles of Wine . . . . Emmylou Harris

Taking a cue from her time as the background singer for Gram Parsons and the Grievous Angels, Harris created the Hot Band, offering sassy, sexy Country Rock in the late 1970s.

Are You Ready for the Country . . . . Neil Young

As well as recording several of his albums on Music Row in Nashville, Young used a lot of Country elements to shape his legendary sound.

WHAT WE SOUND LIKE

One More Night . . . . **Bob Dylan**

No matter what type of music he was fixated on at the time, Dylan remains one of the greatest songwriters ever. This song, from the album, *Nashville Skyline,* was recorded in 1969 in Music City during a time when Dylan was moving away from traditional folk and exploring new styles of expression—including Country.

Tuesday's Gone . . . . **Lynard Skynard**

Known mainly for their southern anthem "Freebird," Skynard's southern charm and rebel attitude later became known as southern rock 'n' roll.

Blue Sky . . . . **The Allman Brothers**

Like Skynard, the Allmans played southern rock 'n' roll—theirs firmly rooted in the blues and guitar playing of Duane Allman and Dickey Betts. This beautiful, upbeat song has deep Country roots sunk in the sounds of Florida swamp blues.

Down on the Corner . . . . **Credence Clearwater Revival**

Even though they formed in California and were known for playing "heartland rock," Credence Clearwater Revival evoked a southern funk in many of their songs, as heard in this classic tune about a New Orleans street dancer.

Dead Flowers . . . . **The Rolling Stones**

Most folks know that the Stones borrowed heavily from the Delta and Country blues, but so too did they borrow from Hank Williams. Here, they are Country to the core.

Space Cowboy . . . . **Widespread Panic**

This contemporary "jam-band" has made a killing with its touring and Grateful Dead-like following. This psychedelic tale of a small-town hippie cowboy reveals their Country roots.

With the Pen in Hand, Master Songwriters:
Singer-Songwriters

They are the storytellers largely responsible for our best Country narratives. Nashville is the last music town left to have a tradition of songwriters who are not also singers. This is a joyfully incomplete list of those who have made a living penning Country songs for themselves and others. New songwriters arrive in town daily, and every year a few good writers become great ones. These artists are poets as well as performers and musicians.

Hard Times. . . . . Stephen Foster

Arguably the first great American songwriter and the author of many classics, including "My Old Kentucky Home," Foster's lyric about the hardships of poverty and labor represents one of the elemental narrative themes of Country.

That's How I Got to Memphis . . . . Tom T. Hall

Hall was nicknamed "The Storyteller," and during the 1960s and 1970s he was considered one of the premier songwriters in Nashville. His songs are simple, humble, singularly descriptive, and have stood the test of time. The legend goes, he wrote many of his songs on bar napkins, while listening to the real world stories of strangers and friends.

Loretta. . . . . Townes Van Zandt

Considered by some to be the best songwriter who ever lived, Van Zandt rejected his privileged, Texas pedigree to explore the life of a rambler and balladeer. His lyrics, like his life, are stark, uncomfortably honest, beautiful, and ultimately tragic, as is the case with this ode to the easiest barroom girl in town.

Angel from Montgomery . . . . John Prine

Simply put, a classic Country song from a master songwriter.

Help Me Make It Through the Night . . . . Kris Kristofferson

Helicopter pilot, Rhode Scholar, songwriter, and actor—Kristofferson is Country's renaissance man. His honest and endearing voice delivers lyrics that are vivid, humble, and heartbreakingly fragile, as demonstrated in this tender plea for temporary shelter from the storm.

MY COUNTRY ROOTS

L.A. Freeway . . . . Guy Clark

A bright star in the pantheon of Texas songwriters, Clark's lyrics can be sweet, brazen, sentimental, and stoic all within a couple lines of verse. He can make you laugh, cry, and leave you wondering which you should do.

Atlantic City . . . . Bruce Springsteen

Although he is known mostly for his contributions as a rock 'n' roll legend, Springsteen borrows from Country in terms of approach to lyric and type of subject matter, especially on his 1982 release, *Nebraska*. This song from that album is a Yankee ballad about the lost hopes and false dreams of a young couple in the gambling capital of the east coast.

Our Town . . . . Iris Dement

Dement's simple, almost provincial lyrics, combined with the awkward twang of her unusual and gorgeous voice, leads you on a hand-held tour through the streets of her hometown and her philosophy of existence.

Family Reserve . . . . Lyle Lovett

One listen to this song about family and the frailty of life will give you a pretty good idea of Lovett's control of the written word. By song's end you feel like a loving member of this crazy West Texas family. His writing always has a way of intimately drawing you in.

Barroom Girls . . . . Gillian Welch

Lyrically and sonically speaking, Welch's songwriting focuses as much attention on what is not there as to what is there. The presence of this negative space allows the listener to ponder and feel her delicate and unadorned lyrics.

Rhonda's Last Ride . . . . Darrell Scott

Scott's strength as a writer comes from his sensitivity and care for his subject matter, and his ability to make the truth beautiful, no matter how dark it might be. This elegy to a prostitute is a perfect example.

Come to Jesus . . . . Mindy Smith

This song, a blessing bestowed from a departed mother to her child, offers wisdom for life, the blessing of death, and the idea that you are never alone. Smith is very young in her career, but her disciplined ability to craft songs assures that songwriting today is being held in careful hands.

I Drink .... **Mary Gauthier**

A songwriter in the finest sense of the word, Gauthier offers a timeless song that explores the standard Country themes of identity, pride, and—what else, but—drinking. A moving delivery on a gorgeous, stirring song. An instant classic.

MY COUNTRY ROOTS

98 Neo-Traditionalists

Beginning in the 1980s, many artists reached back to the traditional arrangements and voices that originally defined Country before the Nashville sound and countrypolitan dominated. Neo-traditionalists are artists who have achieved great commercial success over the past several decades while embracing and celebrating their traditional Country roots. They are as Country as Hank, Faron, or George, and as commercially successful as any who have come before or after. Think pop Country, but with all that great twang.

If It Ain't One Thing (It's You) .... Alan Jackson

Jackson's golden baritone and honest songwriting are akin to a good friend who can comfort you when you are sad and celebrate with you when you are happy. Never hokey, never adulterated, a best of old and new.

She'll Leave You with a Smile .... George Strait

Strait, like Alan Jackson, has become a legend both as a result of his good looks and of his charming baritone voice. He is as nimble playing Texas swing as he is singing a honky tonk ballad.

1982 .... Randy Travis

Like so many in Nashville, Travis moved to town with only his dreams in the early 1980s. Utilizing his legendary bass/baritone voice, traditional arrangements, and a penchant for songs having to do with divorce and broken relationships, it didn't take long for those dreams to come true.

Here's a Quarter (Call Someone Who Cares) .... Travis Tritt

Travis Tritt is George Jones with a biker's sensibility. His voice, like Jones's, can cut you in half with its power and tenderness.

Don't Toss Us Away .... Patty Loveless

Loveless has built a reputation reinterpreting the traditional sounds of Country music. Whether it be a honky tonk two-step or a lonesome bluegrass ballad, her warm alto voice is comfortable in any format.

Killin' Time .... Clint Black

This big-hit from Black, who had five platinum albums in five years, shows how honky tonk twang was smoothed out by the digital recording technologies that emerged in the 1980s. This is stream-lined, chrome-plated Country sounds for the mass-market—but it's Country nonetheless.

He Ought to Know That by Now . . . . **Lee Ann Womack**

If you combined Dolly's delicate vocals, Loretta's spunk, and Tammy's suburban style, you'd have something pretty darnn near Lee Ann Womack.

Whiskey Lullaby . . . . **Brad Paisley (with Alison Krauss)**

Paisley is one of the few modern-day stars that can play his guitar as well as he sings his songs. This duet with Allison Kraus stands toe to toe with any of the great songs in the history of Country. Co-written by old-schooler Bill Anderson and newcomer Jon Randall.

When I Think About Cheating . . . . **Gretchen Wilson**

Wilson is one of the founding members of the "Music Mafia," an underground posse of fringe artists who have promoted and helped one another achieve Country stardom. Echoes of Patsy Cline float about when Wilson gets her voice around a slow tempo ballad as good as this one.

Pocket Full of Gold. . . . . **Vince Gill**

An Oklahoma native, Gill rose through the ranks early in his career as a bluegrass instrumentalist. Building a steady career of number one hits, he has replaced Roy Acuff as the official ambassador for Country music with his highly respected musical chops, a fabulous voice, and an infectious personality.

I'm Not Ready . . . . **Dixie Chicks**

The feisty Texas trio wrote this song in response to the repudiation they faced after making politically-critical comments at a show in London in 2003 that many of their core fans and industry felt were un-American. In true traditional Country spirit, these women never backed down.

Before I Go That Far. . . . . **Elizabeth Cook**

Lush harmonies, traditional arrangements, and simple production, give Cook's music an honesty and immediacy missing from a lot of contemporary Country. She is not one of the genre's most famous singers today, but she is one of the best.

WHAT WE SOUND LIKE

99 Pop

Big Money, Big Sound

Who says Country has to twang? This is a list of some of the major Country artists who are responsible for widening the genre's reach during the past two decades by smoothing-out, but never forgetting, their Country roots while appealing to an increasingly suburban and urban audience

She and I . . . . **Alabama**

When it was all said and done, this group of friends from Fort Payne, Alabama charted thirty-three number one hits. Lush harmonies, power ballads, and raucous stage shows paved the way for such acts as Montgomery Gentry and Rascal Flatts.

Friends in Low Places . . . . **Garth Brooks**

Of the countless number one singles Brooks has recorded, this is his most famous. Brooks was the bridge, stylistically and musically speaking, from the 1980s Country Pop to the Pop that defines Country music today. He turned the concert into a spectacular show—complete with million dollar sets, wireless microphones, and big visual effects. Pop in the way Elvis was Pop, Garth has become something that the King didn't become: a master songwriter.

Cathy's Clown . . . . **Reba McEntire**

This Country legend has sold more than 45 million albums, but you are just as likely to hear synthesizers and digitally generated horns embellish her songs as you are a fiddle or a pedal steel guitar. McEntire is the reigning queen of Country.

Who Invented the Wheel . . . . **Trisha Yearwood**

Citing Linda Ronstadt as a vital influence, Yearwood has made a living scoring number one hits, which sit softly on the mind and easy on the soul. Her string of number one hits in the 1990s paved the way for artists like Faith Hill and Shania Twain to crossover into Pop and Adult Contemporary genres.

Up! . . . . **Shania Twain**

When Twain married Rock/Pop producer Mutt Lange in the early 90s, they collaborated on what became a string of number one hits. These tracks redefined Country pop, what with their catchy hooks, multi-layered effects, and dance remixes that went on to become popular in other non-Country genres. Almost as significant, Shania and music video conspired to make it almost necessary for female Country artists to look like models.

Watch the Wind Blow By . . . . Tim McGraw

Known by his signature black hat and his striking jaw line, McGraw is a new breed of cowboy, one who shops on Rodeo Drive and comfortably incorporates Pop, Hip-Hop, and Soul into his style of Country, as is the case with this song. He is also regarded as one of the best song-pickers in the business.

Concrete Angel . . . . Martina McBride

McBride has one of the biggest and best voices in the music business. Her songs are maternal, delicately delivered, and dramatically produced. She well represents for modern women and their daughters.

Breathe . . . . Faith Hill

Hill represents the modern country girl; one who is as likely to wear an Oscar de la Renta gown as she is to go fishing. Slick production and neutrally crafted "chick" anthems have made her one of the most successful crossover artists in country music today.

Better Life . . . . Keith Urban

The Biker Poet. This Australia native is good looking, easy on the ears, and one hell of a guitar player. His songs can be optimistic, sympathetic, and sensitive, as well as hard driving and rowdy. He's a guy's guy who the girls can't keep their eyes off of.

You Had Me from Hello . . . . Kenny Chesney

Think Jimmy Buffett and John Cougar Mellencamp with a good dose of Tennessee pride. Slick videos, well-written songs, and the casual close-up have made Chesney a Country pop icon.

How Do You Like Me Now . . . . Toby Keith

Part outlaw, part patriot, and part comedian, Keith has solidified his place as the voice of the suburban country male. He uses a dramatic, often intimidating baritone voice to deliver songs that celebrate male pride and the machismo spirit of Country.

Coming to Your City . . . . Big & Rich

The hippy, hick-hop stars of contemporary Country. Big & Rich are bringing their music to your town now—spreading peace, love, hip-hop-styled lyrics, banjo licks and a rousing "yee-haw." Some might consider them today's version of the early comedian musicians like Uncle Dave Macon and Stringbean, what with all their shenanigans.

WHAT WE SOUND LIKE

My Maria . . . .**Brooks & Dunn**

These guys were the biggest Country duo of the 1990s. Ronnie Dunn's voice has a special effect on the female heart and the Brooks-led band's hard-driving sound evokes the male outlaw spirit. As a result, they have become one of the leaders of the modern Country pop sound.

The Broken Road. . . . . **Rascal Flatts**

A beautiful ballad and a huge hit, written by A-list writers, Bobby Boyd, Jeff Hanna and Marcus Hummon about the crooked, imperfect roads that lead us to love. An example of Country pop in which powerful songwriting isn't lost in big-budget, mass-market production.

100 Alternative Country

Outlaw Revisited

When Country becomes so pop that you can't recognize it as Country, anything resembling older Country becomes alternative Country. Strange, but true. Here is a going-on-the-space-shuttle-and-I-only-have-money-for-twelve-downloads-alt-country playlist. These artists pride themselves on being fine songwriters, live on the margins of the mainstream, and much like the outlaws, represent outsider country.

South Nashville Blues . . . . .Steve Earle

Earle cites Texas blues legend Mance Lipscomb and songwriter Townes Van Zandt as big influences on his sound. His music is singularly poetic, stubborn, complexly-conceived, and often politically driven.

Essence . . . . .Lucinda Williams

As a native of Mississippi, Williams worked her way onto the scene playing the country blues native to her state. By merging the rhythms of the blues with a languid and poetic repertoire, she has become one of the leaders on the alternative Country scene.

Give Back the Key to My Heart . . . . Uncle Tupelo

This band is credited with producing the sound that became known as "Alternative Country." Their lo-fi Country music was influenced as much by elements of Rock 'n' Roll as by punk music. Uncle Tupelo only released a few albums before the members split up to form the bands Wilco and Son Volt.

Come Pick Me Up . . . . Ryan Adams

Originally the lead singer of the band "Whiskeytown," Adams is a prolific writer who is as famous for his outlaw attitude as he is for his songwriting. Many consider his album, *Heartbreaker*, which this song appears on, to be an alt-country masterpiece.

Waiting for the Sun . . . . .The Jayhawks

More Rock 'n' Roll than Country, this Minnesota band made several critically-acclaimed albums before disbanding a few years ago. Their compelling narratives and high harmonies contribute to their alternative Country identity.

WHAT WE SOUND LIKE

You're Still on My Mind . . . . **Freakwater**

This honky tonk band from Kentucky showcases lazy, two-part female harmonies and, often dark, gothic lyrics.

Georgia Hard . . . . **Robbie Fulks**

Fulks is the leader of Chicago's postmodern Country community. Like so many, he came to Nashville early in his career but was rejected by the decision-makers on Music Row. As this song demonstrates, he is one of the great songwriters and performers that Country music has to offer.

Nashville . . . . **Todd Snider**

Snider is one of the most prolific and acclaimed singer-songwriters you've probably never heard of. He's equal parts honky tonk, hipster, and beatnik poet. It's safe to say people will be listening to his music long after his time.

Painting Her Fingernails . . . . **Bare Jr.**

The son of 1950s country legend, Bobby Bare, blends elements of punk, rock, and Country to create a sound truly his own. Here, he covers one of Shel Silverstein's legendary country ballads.

If It Runs . . . . **Bad Livers**

Some have called the Bad Livers "Thrash Bluegrass" for their raucous, heavy metal interpretation of the genre. Their records are brash, bawdy, and unapologetic

Winter's Song . . . . **Cowboy Junkies**

One of the songs that made this Canadian band of siblings famous was a cover of Hank Williams's, "I'm So Lonesome I Could Cry." Since then, they have continued to refine their sound with their own version of Country soul.

List of Reasons . . . . **Dale Watson**

This Austin, Texas local hero's sound conjures Merle Haggard, but with a deeper voice. Watson has never been accepted by the Nashville mainstream community and thus has always been considered alternative, even though he is one of the great honky tonk writers and singers in all of Country music.

FILMS

Some movies are a lot like a great big complicated Country song. The following are arguably the 100 best movies that contain, act like, inspire, are inspired by, or reflect the aesthetics of Country. To get a sense of the movie, note the playlist or playlists indicated. Following the 100 films is a short list of our favorite Country documentaries. Sometimes listening just isn't enough.

THE APOSTLE
86. God, 47. Cheating, 34. Hard Questions, 84. Simple Wisdom, 82. Irony

ALICE DOESN'T LIVE HERE ANYMORE
13. Feminist, 19. Waitresses, 4. Ramblers, 77. Good Love, 68. Music Industry

A STREET CAR NAMED DESIRE
42. Crazy, 48. Hot, 1. Honky Tonk Angels, 14. Ladies of Legend

ALL THE KING'S MEN
15. Mythic Men

A SOLDIER'S STORY
18. Soldiers, 10. Black

BABE
74. Kids

BASTARD OUT OF CAROLINA
33. Abuse

BLOOD SIMPLE
39. Murder, 24. Cheating, 82. Irony

BONNIE AND CLYDE
5. Outlaws/Bandits, 79. Love and the Road

BOUND FOR GLORY
15. Mythic Men, 68. Music Industry

BREAKING AWAY
58. Country Contrasted, 72. Family, 83. Labor

BULL DURHAM
28. Courting

BUTCH CASSIDY AND THE SUNDANCE KID
5. Outlaws/ Bandits

BEST LITTLE WHOREHOUSE IN TEXAS
7. Hookers, 14. Ladies of Legend, 48. Hot, 65. United State of Texas

CAT ON A HOT TIN ROOF
72. Family, 23. Love and Money, 44. Existential Despair, 43. Country Erotica, 47. Love Hurts

COAL MINER'S DAUGHTER
68. Music Industry, 3. Good Women, 13. Feminist, 14. Ladies of Legend, 32. Coal Mining

COME BACK TO THE FIVE AND DIME, JIMMY DEAN, JIMMY DEAN
12. Teen Girls, 22. Old People, 43. Haunted

COOL HAND LUKE
31. Jails and Prisons, 21. Icons, 15. Mythic Men, 5. Outlaws/Bandits

DAYS OF HEAVEN
59. Poverty, 23. Love and Money, 43. Country Erotica, 83. Labor

DEADMAN WALKING
40. Executions, 86. God

DELIVERANCE
8. Rednecks, 39. Murder, 49. Revenge, 33. Abuse

DIVINE SECRETS OF THE YA-YA SISTERHOOD
6. Bad Mamas

DRIVING MISS DAISY
10. Black

EAST OF EDEN
6. Bad Mamas, 72. Family, 86. God

EASY RIDER
4. Ramblers, 61. Roads, 37. Drugs

FRIED GREEN TOMATOES
33. Abuse, 39. Murder, 3. Good Women, 60. Coffee, Cigarettes, & Sugar, 10. Black, 86. God

FORREST GUMP
73. Mama, 81. History, 82. Irony, 16. Fools, 1. Honky Tonk Angels, 33. Abuse, 51. Surreal, 35. Sweet Invitations

GEORGIA
68. Music Industry, 72. Family, 36. Alcohol

THE GRAPES OF WRATH
59. Poverty, 72. Family, 71. Spirit, 4. Ramblers, 64. California

THE GUNFIGHTER
5. Outlaws/Bandits, 21. Icons

HARRY AND TONTO
22.Old People, 61. Roads

HIGH NOON
20. Cowboys, 3. Good Women

HONKYTONK MAN
2. Honky Tonk Men

HONEYSUCKLE ROSE
15. Mythic Men, 68. Music Industry, 61. Roads, 4. Ramblers, 36. Alcohol, 37. Drugs, 35. Sweet Invitations

HUSH, HUSH, SWEET CHARLOTTE
42. Crazy, 39.Murder, 53. Haunted, 56.Hometown

I AM A FUGITIVE FROM A CHAIN GANG
31. Jails and Prisons

IN THE HEAT OF THE NIGHT
39. Murder, 10. Black

IT'S A WONDERFUL LIFE
84. Simple Wisdom, 77. Good Love

JAIL HOUSE ROCK
31. Jails and Prisons, 26. Dance with the Devil, 68. Music Industry

JEZEBEL
78. Loving Lies, 14. Ladies of Legend

LAST PICTURE SHOW
12. Teen Girls, 20. Cowboys, 56. Hometown, 47. Love Hurts, 54. Last Call

LILLIES OF THE FIELD
11. John Henry

THE LITTLE FOXES
23. Love and Money, 39. Murder, 72. Family

THE LITTLEST REBEL
66. Return South/Lost South, 10. Black, 74. Kids

THE LONG, HOT SUMMER
46. Desire, 4. Ramblers, 8. Rednecks, 15. Mythic Men, 17. Mamas and Daddies, 72. Family, 76. Married Love

LOVE ME TENDER
68. Music Industry, 18. Soldiers, 77. Good Love

MAGNOLIA 60
51. Surreal, 86. God, 72. Family, 44. Existential Despair

MATEWAN
32.Coal Mining

McCABE AND MRS. MILLER
7. Hooker, 5.Outlaws/Bandits, 20.Cowboys

MEMBER OF THE WEDDING
12. Teen Girls

MIDNIGHT COWBOY
63. Big City, 75. Friends, 79. Love and the Road, 7. Hookers, 85. Death

MY DARLING CLEMENTINE
20. Cowboys

NASHVILLE
67. Music Row, 68. Music Industry, 69. Cities, 52. Country Is Identity

NINE TO FIVE
83. Labor, 13. Feminist

NORMA RAE
83. Labor

O BROTHER, WHERE ART THOU
61. Roads, 89. Bluegrass, 72. Mythic Men, 31. Jails and Prisons

OTHER VOICES, OTHER ROOMS
22. Old People, 72. Family, 56. Hometown, 51. Surreal, 53. Haunted

PARIS, TEXAS
65. The United State of Texas, 68. Music Industry, 50. Before & After the "Big D"

PEGGY SUE GOT MARRIED
12. Teen Girls, 77. Good Love, 3. Good Women, 76. Married Love

PICNIC
12. Teen Girls, 48. Hot, 43. Country Erotica, 4. Ramblers, 78. Loving Lies

PLACES IN THE HEART
3. Good Women, 11. John Henry, 10. Black, 83. Labor

PLATOON
18. Soldiers, 75. Friends

FILMS

PRINCE OF TIDES
42. Crazy, 56. Hometown, 55. Home, 72. Family, 73. Mama, 6. Bad Mamas

PURE COUNTRY
68. Music Industry, 58. Country Contrasted, 76. Married Love

RED RIVER
20. Cowboy, 57. Mountain River, 61. Roads, 86. God

REFLECTIONS IN A GOLDEN EYE
24. Cheating, 51. Surreal, 18. Soldiers

RHINESTONE
68. Music Industry

ROADIE
75. Friends, 68. Music Industry

SATURDAY NIGHT LIGHTS
29. Rings, 65. The United States of Texas, 17. Mamas & Daddies, 21. Icons, 75. Friends

THE SEARCHERS
40. Executions, 5. Outlaws/Bandits, 9. Angels, 34. Hard Questions.

SERGEANT YORK
81. History, 18. Soldiers

SHANE
20. Cowboys, 5. Outlaws/Bandits, 34. Hard Questions, 85. Death

SHAWSHANK REDEMPTION
31. Jails and Prisons, 75. Friends, 49. Revenge, 26. Dance with the Devil

SLING BLADE
39. Murder, 33. Abuse, 72. Family, 68. Music Industry

SMOKEY AND THE BANDIT
61. Roads

SMOOTH TALK
12. Teen Girls

SONGCATCHER
68.Music Industry, 13. Feminist

SPITFIRE GRILL
31. Jails and Prisons, 18. Soldiers, 19. Waitresses, 73. Mama, 71. Spirit

SPLENDOR IN THE GRASS
12. Teen Girls, 58. Country Contrasted, 42. Crazy, 43. Country Erotica,
53. Haunted, 25. Goodbye Love, 41. Love Begs

STAND BY ME
75. Friends, 74. Kids, 4. Ramblers

STEEL MAGNOLIAS
1. Honky Tonk Angels, 3. Good Women, 9. Angels, 73. Mama,
14. Ladies of Legend

SUGARLAND EXPRESS
17. Mamas & Daddies, 5. Outlaws/Bandits, 61. Roads

SWEET BIRD OF YOUTH
4. Ramblers, 9. Angels, 16. Fools, 62. Motels, 22. Old People,
36. Alcohol, 37. Drugs

SWEET DREAMS
68. Music Industry

SWEET HOME ALABAMA
56. Hometown, 77. Good Love

TARNISHED ANGELS
75. Friends, 3. Good Women, 46. Desire

TENDER MERCIES
68. Music Industry, 72. Family, 2. Honky Tonk Men

THELMA AND LOUISE
75. Friends, 61. Roads, 13. Feminist

THEY SHOOT HORSES, DON'T THEY?
59. Poverty

THING CALLED LOVE
67. Music Row, 68. Music Industry

TO KILL A MOCKINGBIRD
10. Black, 15. Mythic Men, 16. Fools, 31. Jails and Prisons, 8. Rednecks

TOBACCO ROAD
59. Poverty, 8. Rednecks

TRUE GRIT
22. Old People, 20. Cowboys, 5. Outlaws, 15. Mythic Men, 21. Icons

UNFORGIVEN
5. Outlaws/Bandits, 22. Old People, 7. Hookers, 72. Family, 49. Revenge

URBAN COWBOY
1. Honky Tonk Angels, 2. Honky Tonk Men, 68. Music Industry

THE YEARLING
74. Kids, 72. Family

WALK THE LINE
68. Music Industry

THE WESTERNER
20. Cowboys, 5. Outlaws

WISE BLOOD
86. God, 39. Murder, 80. Mama Earth

THE WILD BUNCH
5. Outlaws, 20. Cowboys, 54. Last Call

WOODSTOCK
80. Mama Earth, 96. Country Rock, 81. History

The Documentaries

BE HERE TO LOVE ME: A FILM ABOUT TOWNES VAN ZANDT
Directed by Margaret Brown

HARLAN COUNTY U.S.A.
Barbara Kopple's Oscar-winning documentary about coal mining in Kentucky.

HEART WORN HIGHWAYS
Texas poets. Townes van Zandt, Guy Clark, Steve Earle. Rodney Crowell. Susanna Clark. Texas singer/songwriters at home but in exile somewhere near Nashville.

HIGH LONESOME
Bluegrass documentary.

HANK WILLIAMS: HONKY TONK BLUES
PBS American Masters series.

LOUISIANA HAYRIDE
The story of the "other" Opry that birthed such greats as Hank Williams and Elvis Presley.

NO DIRECTION HOME
Martin Scorcese's documentary on Bob Dylan.

WILL THE CIRCLE BE UNBROKEN
PBS American Experience.

MY COUNTRY ATLAS

An Idiosyncratic Guide To Country Inspired Travels

Get the details from your favorite travel sites. Mapquest, Yahoo maps, and Google are all great. Double check all our details. Treat this like a series of post-its from defunct cousins living in Music City.

What Are The Three Great Cities Of Country Music?

Nashville, Tennessee; Austin, Texas; Bakersfield, California

When In Nashville, Tennessee, Music City U.S.A., Don't Miss:

The Ryman Auditorium
The Country Music Hall of Fame
Hatch Show Print
RCA Studio B
The Grand Ole Opry House
Jubilee Hall, Fisk University
Gruhn Guitars
The Bluebird Café
Tootsie's Orchid Lounge
Bobby's Idle Hour
Robert's Western World
Martha's at the Plantation
Manuel's

And If You Have An Extra Day To Drive A Few Hours West And South To Memphis, Tennessee, Don't Miss:

Graceland
Sun Records
Peabody Hotel
Ribs at the Rendezvous Restaurant

When In Austin Texas, The Live Music Capital Of The World, Don't Miss:

South by Southwest (every March)
6th Street Clubs
Driscoll Hotel
Barton Springs
Drinks at The Four Seasons
University of Texas, *Austin City Limits* taping

When In Bakersfield, California, Land Of Owens, Haggard, & Yoakam, Don't Miss:

Kern County Museum (3801 Chester Avenue, 661 852 5000)
Buck Owens' Crystal Palace
Best Western next to the Crystal Palace
Trout's (a Honky Tonk)
Dinner at the Noriega Hotel

Three Great Country Regions:

Appalachia, Texas Hill country, Mississippi Delta

Best Cool Country Venues:

The Birchmere, Alexandria, Virginia
Gruene Hall, New Braunfels, Texas
Billy Bob's, Fort Worth, Texas
Arkey Blue's Silver Dollar Bar Bandera, Texas
The Ryman Auditorium, Nashville, Tennessee
The Station Inn, Nashville, Tennessee

Best Country Festivals:

FAN FAIR (CMA MUSIC FESTIVAL), June, Nashville
SOUTH BY SOUTHWEST, March, Austin, Texas
KERRVILLE FOLK FESTIVAL, May - June, Kerrville, Texas
MERLEFEST, April, Wilkesboro, North Carolina
BONNAROO, June, Manchester, Tennessee
BROOKLYN COUNTRY MUSIC FESTIVAL, September, New York, New York
APPALACHIAN STRING BAND MUSIC FESTIVAL, August, Clifftop, West Virginia

Want To Visit A Town Dear To The Country Heart? Try:

Bristol, Tennessee
Ralph Peer first recorded Jimmie Rodgers and the Carter Family in Bristol.
Muscle Shoals, Alabama
Considered the crossroad between Country and R & B. Visit Fame Studios.
Montgomery, Alabama
Burial place of Hank Williams, 1305 Upper Wetumpka Road.

Want To Visit The Hometown Of A Country Great? Here Are A Few:

Roy Acuff, Maynardville, Tennessee
Amede Ardoin, near Lafayette, Louisiana

MY COUNTRY ROOTS

Chet Atkins, Luttrell, Tennessee
Owen Bradley, Westmoreland, Tennessee
Glen Campbell, Delight, Arkansas
A.P. Carter, Mace's Spring Virginia,
Maybelle Carter, Nicklesville, Virginia
Johnny Cash, Kingsland, Arkansas
Don Everly, Brownie, Kentucky
Lester Flatt, Duncan's Chapel, Tennessee
Lefty Frizzell, Corsicana, Texas
Merle Haggard, Bakersfield, California
Harland Howard, Detroit, Michigan
Waylon Jennings, Littlefield, Texas
George Jones, Saratoga, Texas
Kris Kristofferson, Brownsville, Texas
Loretta Lynn, Butcher Hollow, Kentucky
Roger Miller, Fort Worth, Texas
Patsy Montana, Hope, Arkansas
Willie Nelson, Abbott, Texas
Buck Owens, Sherman, Texas
Minnie Pearl, Centerville, Tennessee
Ralph Peer, Kansas City, Missouri
Sam Phillips, Florence, Alabama
Web Pierce, West Monroe, Louisiana
Elvis Presley, Tupelo, Mississippi
Ray Price, Perryville, Texas
Charley Pride, Sledge, Mississippi
Earl Scruggs, Flint Hill, North Carolina
Jim Reeves, Panola County, Texas
Tex Ritter, Panola County, Texas
Jimmie Rodgers, Meridian, Mississippi
Fred Rose, Evansville, Indiana
Wesley Rose, Chicago, Illinois
Conway Twitty, Friars Point, Mississippi
Kitty Wells, Nashville, Tennessee
Hank Williams, Mount Olive, Alabama
Bob Wills, Kosse, Texas

Looking For Country In The Big Apple?

Tour Central Park and remember Garth's Concert. The largest in the Park's history.

In 2006, these clubs served up Country at least some of the time:

Rodeo Bar, 375 3rd Avenue at 27th Street
Bowery Ballroom, 6 Delancey

Parkside Lounge (Monday nights), 317 E. Houston at Attorney Street, Manhattan

Baggot Inn, 82 W. 3rd Street at Sullivan, Manhattan

Hank's Saloon, 46 3rd Avenue at Atlantic Avenue, Brooklyn

Lakeside Lounge, 162 Avenue B at E.10th Street, Manhattan (Try the jukebox.)

Trailer Park Lounge, 271 W 23rd between 7th and 8th Avenue (Comfort food, southern white style.)

Want To Learn More About The World Of Country Music While Reading A Murder Mystery Written By A Country Legend Who Sometimes Lives In New York? Try:

A Case of Lone Star or *Road Kill* written by Kinky Friedman. Nashville-based writers Cecelia Tishy and Steven Womack have also published interesting murder mysteries involving the world of country music.

Want To Visit A Coal Mine? Check Out:

Pocahontas Exhibition Coal Mine and Museum Pocahontas, West Virginia

Beckley Exhibition Coal Mine Beckley, West Virginia

Want To Learn To Write A Country Song? Try:

Old Town School of Folk Music, Chicago, Illinois

Want To Have A Close Encounter With A Movie Cowboy, Or Just Longing For Country In Los Angeles? Visit:

The Gene Autry Museum of Western Heritage

Want Your Own Close Encounter With Country?

Ride a Greyhound bus—anywhere but especially, North to South or South to North, or way out West. Or, ride in a vintage Cadillac. Eat a homegrown tomato. Download a new list to your mp3 player.

Want To Cook Southern?

Buy, read, and cook from John Egerton's *Southern Food*. It is our bible of southern cooking.

Want To Eat Southern Food As Elegant, Pure, And Real As Emmylou Harris' Voice? Try:

Highland's Grill, Birmingham, Alabama, for the perfect "fancy" southern meal, the best in America.

ABOUT THE AUTHORS

Carter Little is a professional songwriter, composer, and performer living in Nashville, Tennessee. Having fronted many Country bands over the past fifteen years, he recently released his second solo album, *Dare To Be Small*, to critical acclaim, and notably completed a debut film score for the feature *The Living Wake*.

Alice Randall has had songs recorded by a range of country artists from Glen Campbell and Trisha Yearwood to Marie Osmond and Steve Earle. She wrote a video for Reba MacIntire that was ACM video of the year. A member of ASCAP's Number One Club and a New York Times bestselling novelist, Alice Randall is Writer in Residence at Vanderbilt University where she teaches a course in Country Music Lyrics as Literature. Randall is a screenwriter and frequent contributor to *Elle Magazine* and has contributed to both the *Los Angeles Times* and *O Magazine*.

Courtney Little is a singer-songwriter who resides in Nashville. Prior to moving to Music City, Little lived in NYC and worked for Oscar Award-winning documentarian, Ken Burns. He recently released his third album, *Children's Music*, under the pseudonym Samuel Springs. While he favors Haggard, his chocolate lab, Celia, prefers Loretta through and through.

INDEX BY ARTIST

INDEX BY ARTIST

INDEX BY ARTIST

INDEX BY ARTIST

INDEX BY ARTIST

INDEX BY ARTIST

INDEX BY ARTIST

INDEX BY ARTIST

INDEX BY ARTIST

INDEX BY ARTIST

INDEX BY ARTIST

MY COUNTRY ROOTS

INDEX BY ARTIST

INDEX BY ARTIST

INDEX BY ARTIST